Miss-representation

PETER LANG
PROMPT

PETER LANG
Oxford • Bern • Berlin • Bruxelles • New York • Wien

Clare Gorman (editor)

Miss-representation

Women, Literature, Sex and Culture

PETER LANG
Oxford • Bern • Berlin • Bruxelles • New York • Wien

Bibliographic information published by **Die Deutsche Nationalbibliothek**.
Die Deutsche Nationalbibliothek lists this publication in the "Deutsche Nationalbibliografie"; detailed bibliographic data are available on the Internet at http://dnb.d-nb.de/.

A catalogue record for this book is available from the British Library.

Library of Congress Cataloging-in-Publication Data
Names: Gorman, Clare, author of preface.
Title: Miss-representation : women : literature, sex and culture / Clare Gorman [preface].
Description: Oxford ; New York : Peter Lang, 2020. | Includes bibliographical references and index.
Identifiers: LCCN 2020016869 (print) | LCCN 2020016870 (ebook) | ISBN 9781788745864 (hardback) | ISBN 9781788745871 (ebook) | ISBN 9781788745888 (epub) | ISBN 9781788745895 (mobi)
Subjects: LCSH: Sex role--Ireland. | Social role--Ireland. | Women--Ireland--Social conditions.
Classification: LCC HQ1075.5.I73 M57 2020 (print) | LCC HQ1075.5.I73 (ebook) | DDC 305.309417--dc23
LC record available at https://lccn.loc.gov/2020016869
LC ebook record available at https://lccn.loc.gov/2020016870

ISBN 978-1-78874-586-4 (print) • ISBN 978-1-78874-587-1 (ePDF)
ISBN 978-1-78874-588-8 (ePub) • ISBN 978-1-78874-589-5 (mobi)

Published by Peter Lang Ltd, International Academic Publishers, 52 St Giles, Oxford, OX1 3LU, United Kingdom
oxford@peterlang.com, www.peterlang.com

This publication has been peer reviewed.

For Women

Contents

Figures

MARY MCAULIFFE

Foreword

In 2017, I attended a conference run under the auspices of the Women On Ireland Research Network entitled 'Women and Irishness' at Waterford Institute of Technology (WIT) in Waterford city. The theme of the conference was premised on using the centenary of the Easter Rising in Ireland to ask questions of gender, women and femininity and how they intersect with the idea of Irishness. This symposium aimed to bring together current scholarly work critiquing female experiences, how women are represented in culture, media, and socialization through the lens of an Irish experience. Over two packed days, there were panels on topics ranging from sports/leisurewear, porn, sex, sex education, women and ageing, gender in the culinary arts, women in science, to the underrepresentation of sportswomen in the mass media. Keynotes were delivered by Professor Louise Ryan (University of Sheffield), on stories of Irish migrants to London; Professor Ann Fogarty (University College Dublin), on contemporary Irish women's writing, specifically looking at the writer Eimear McBride and the idea of women and identity within McBride's work; Dr Máire Leane (University College Cork), on the representation of adolescent female sexuality in Ireland; and Dr Mary Condren (Trinity College Dublin), questioning the depictions of women as angels or sinister temptresses within mythologies.

While not all attendees at the conference were academic or early career scholars, it was to the credit of the organizers that the final panel (on which I participated) spoke to the underrepresentation of women in senior positions within the third-level system in Ireland. There was a very lively discussion regarding the reasons this imbalance still exists and what we need to do to rectify it. Many conferences such as this leave one buzzing with new ideas, thinking of ways to continue research and activism within and outside of the academy, as well feeling the solidarity of spending time among those who understand the importance of viewing all issues through a gendered lens. However, the event often fades into memory as more conferences and more challenges arise. This is why I am particularly delighted to see that a publication is now coming from the 2017 'Women and Irishness' event, and even more honoured to have been asked to write a foreword for it. There are many ways of thinking of women and Irishness – oftentimes it is the challenges that Irish women have endured through the last 100 years that are discussed. We often, by necessity, read about the Mother and Baby Homes, Magdalen Laundries, the exclusion of Traveller women, migrant women, working-class women from specific definitions of Irishness. However, other aspects of women and Irishness can and should be unpacked.

For all their disparate subject matters, a solid link that connects the five essays in this volume is gender. From Mary Farrell's in-depth study of the gendered work environment in the Irish chef profession, through to Isobel Ní Riain's discussion of the role of female empowerment and sexuality in Nuala Ní Dhomhaill, these essays touch on concerns of representation, inclusion, and gender activism. The other essays similarly deal with issues of sexual consent, educational equality and the representation and portrayal of women in the media. A woman I have long been fascinated with is Louise Gavan Duffy, who embodied the campaigns for equality; an educator, nationalist and Irish-language enthusiast, she was involved in campaigns for female suffrage, Irish freedom and Irish-language education. Celia de Fréine's chapter on Gavan Duffy shines a new light on the work of this important woman.

Based on detailed surveys, Mary Farrell's and Yvonne Murphy's chapter open up the world of chef work and consent respectively. Delving deep into one of the biggest industries in Ireland, Farrell's original research forefronts the underrepresentation in the industry, especially at senior levels. Murphy's invaluable research demonstrates that as women mature, they gain a better understanding of and more confidence in concepts of consent. This begs the question of how we need to inculcate this confidence in younger women, so they too can be confident around consent. The never-ending questions around how women are portrayed in the media are central to Brenda Murphy's essay. Women as commodities, fetishized or hypersexualized, women as victims, as others – the continuing objectification of the female body in the media is impressively drawn out by Murphy.

Ní Riain's discussion on the poetry of Ní Dhomhaill shows also the questioning of the status quo, both in terms of gender and language. The links between the disparate essays is the centring on women, work and activism. The research and analysis here – on women in chef work, representation in the media, attitudes to sexual consent, and the use of poetry and literature, education and the Irish language to question the status quo – are important in our understanding of women within Irish society. What has been achieved and what still needs to be achieved?

It was my pleasure to attend and participate in the 2017 conference from which this collection stems and it has been my pleasure to read and introduce these chapters, which unpack many vital issues relating to gender and Irishness.

CLARE GORMAN

Preface

If asked to describe this edited collection, I would say that it is a book written by women on a variety of different topics pertaining to women. What unfolds between the covers of this book are essays which are strong on the diverse ways in which gender, radical discrimination and women daring to be different are rooted within themes like culture, media, education, and literature. This edited collection brings together the research of five women on a variety of different subject areas, from gendered roles within the chef profession to patriarchy and striptease culture. These chapters are vastly different in their themes, but united in the fact that they offer discussions on the roles, representations and perceptions of women from the early 1900s to the present day. The innovative and originality of this book dwells in the fact that the chapters are written by the feminine on various subjects appertaining to women, giving the collection an all-female narrative and space. The overall aim of the book is to seamlessly blend the research being carried out on barriers, challenges, and dilemmas experienced by women in our society.

Chapter 1 provides an inquiry into female chefs, their roles and working environments in the professional culinary world. For 'all restaurants employ cooks; however, higher-end restaurants and upscale hotels employ both cooks and chefs. Chefs are the "chiefs" of the kitchen and they are expected to manage both the kitchen and its staff, as well as hold creative control over the kitchen'; they are essentially the stanchion, that are necessary for the successful running of any kitchen (Harris and Giuffre 2015). However, why has the chef profession been dominated by men? This question is the motivation behind Mary Farrell's chapter entitled 'The gendered roles and work environments in the chef profession in Ireland'. Indeed, Farrell is investigating the gendered stratification of roles and work environments in the chef profession in Ireland. This chapter is centred around a survey

Farrell carried out between October 2016 and December 2016, *Step up to the Plate, Gender Inequality in the Chef Profession in Ireland*, which postulates why are there an underrepresentation of women within the chef profession, especially when it comes to women holding head chef leadership roles. The central argument of this chapter is clear: there are not enough women making it to the top of the chef industry and why is this? Over the past number of years, only a few women have managed to smash this gendered boundary. For instance, Danni Barry, Ireland's only female Michelin-star chef, the Kemp sisters, Peaches and Domini, Darina Allen and her daughter in-law Rachel, to name but a few. However, as the head chef at Macnean House, Blackloin, Co. Cavan, puts it, 'it's an ongoing challenge to inspire and promote the great work that women continue to achieve in the food industry in Ireland' (Valadeau, 2019).

Chapter 2 examines the concept of sexual consent, specifically how sexual consent is a concept that evolves for individuals as they age in terms of both comprehension and the language used to describe this topic. Yvonne Murphy's chapter outlines how she conducted a qualitative research project, where eight women aged between 26 to 62, chosen through snowballing sampling, were interviewed in order to ascertain their relationship with sexual consent. Murphy describes how the relationship status of the women varied from single, polyamorous, in a relationship, married, married with children and widowed, giving the study a profoundness and spanning across multiple perspectives. All the women were living in Ireland at the time, but not all were originally from Ireland. This conversation of sexual consent was intertwined with the theory of liminality and a feminist postmodern approach was taken within this chapter. Indeed, the overarching outcomes Murphy ascertained are that the women's understanding of consent is something that has matured over time and they have a better understanding of sexual consent at their current age than during their teenage years. Cradled over a decade ago by Tarana Burke, who initially started the '#MeToo' campaign, men and women are now speaking out about their experiences of sexual consent, sexual harassment, unwanted sexual advancements, and how we communicate sexual consent. Murphy's chapter, entitled 'Sexual consent: Are the lines really that blurred?' opens an imperative discussion on this topic.

It can be argued that nineteen- and twentieth-century reflections of women have been stained by patriarchy, oppression, lacking opportunity outside the home, essentially fulfilling the previously held article 41.2 of the constitution of Ireland, which deems a woman's place to be within the home. Indeed, women either worked in factories or were confined to domestic work. However, the end of the nineteenth century and the early twentieth century saw women raising their voices and fighting for one thing – equality. The war on men advancing and women were now demanding equal opportunity in all expressions of life. One such change maker and truly influential women is described in Celia de Fréine chapter, entitled 'The woman who would teach Irish'. Chapter 3 looks at the life of Louise Gavan Duffy. This was a women who altered the landscape of the education system by co-founding, along with Eithne McAodha, *Scoil Bhríde* [St Brigid's School], the first *Gaelscoil* [all-Irish primary school] in Dublin. This chapter describes Louise Gavan Duffy's life and the events that led her to reshape the face of the education system by concieving the idea of teaching all subjects through the Irish language.

The European Platform of Regulatory Authority (EPRA) conducted and published a report in September of 2018 looking at the representation of women in audiovisual media industry. The overall findings suggest women are less likely to appear as experts in scientific or technical roles. In the UK only 26 per cent of technical and engineering roles are held by women and there appears to be a 'glass ceiling' which prevents women from accessing especially technical and leadership/decision making jobs (European Commission, 2019). And when it comes to on-screen portrayals, women appear less, but when they do women are subject to more stereotypical portrayals than men (European Commission, 2019). We are familiar with the female as a supermom, the strong corporate climber, the blonde sexy type in need of a rich husband and so on. Indeed, Chapter 4 by Brenda Murphy, entitled 'Media landscapes and striptease cultures: Patriarchy, portrayal and bodies', opens up a conversation regarding how women are portrayed in the media. For Murphy, our print, social and web media is fuelled by patriarchal ideologies which portray women as commodified, hypersexualized; they are falling victim to, as Murphy puts it, 'patriarchal discursive practices' – men holding power over women. We turn on the

TV, browse the web, scroll through our social media, Facebook/Twitter/ Instagram – there is a good chance we will encounter gendered stereotypes of women. This chapter discusses how the media objectifies and eroticizes the female entity.

In Chapter 5, Isobel Ní Riain discusses 'Nuala Ní Dhomhnaill's poetic women'. Ní Dhomhnaill is one of Ireland's famous Irish poets. She studied Irish and English at University College Cork in 1969 and became a member of the Irish-language poetry movement. For Ní Dhomhnaill, the Irish language has become an integral part of her identity, culture and self-expression. She was the first Professor of Irish-language Poetry, and chooses to share her lyrical expression only through the medium of Irish (Gaelic). Ní Riain focuses specifically on the role of the female, the feminine, female empowerment, and the notion of female sexuality within Ní Dhomhnaill's poetry, which is derived from ancient Irish folklore. Indeed, Ní Riain opens up the conversation regarding Ní Dhomhnaill and her questioning of the status quo in her poetry, which is presented in both Irish and English.

Bibliography

European Commission (2018). 'EPRA Survey results (focus on ERGA members) Achieving greater diversity in broadcasting – special focus on gender'. *Working Report on Gender Representation in the Audiovisual Media Sector.* <https://ec.europa.eu/digital-single-market/en/news/working-report-gender-representation-audiovisual-media-sector>, accessed 30 September 2019.

Harris, Deborah A., and Giuffre, Patti (2015). *Taking the Heat: Women Chefs and Gender Inequality in the Professional Kitchen.* New Brunswick, NJ: Rutgers University Press.

Valadeau, K. (2019). 'Women of the Irish Food Industry'. *Proper Food.* <http://www.properfood.ie/carmel-mcguirr-macnean-house/>, accessed 10 September 2019.

MARY FARRELL

1 The gendered roles and work environments in the chef profession in Ireland

The chef world is a curious culinary conundrum, where women have made steady but limited progress in the historically male-dominated chef profession since the 1960s, while they remain the predominant home cooks in contemporary society in Ireland. Furthermore, researchers suggest that women's roles within the profession are stratified along gender lines, where they may occupy specific 'feminine' *pastry chef* roles or lower-grade *commis chef* roles; there is, however, a notable lack of females in the most common leadership role of *head chef* (Farrell 2016; Harris and Giuffre 2015). In addition, research suggests that men and women occupy different work environments, where women tend to work more in day-time service professional kitchens, while men are found in full-service restaurants (Harris and Giuffre 2015; Lutario 2010).

Over the course of my twenty-five-year career as a chef, I have often wondered why the chef profession has been dominated by men.[1] However, the lack of comprehensive quantitative data was a critical limiting factor in my ability to assess the extent of gender inequality within the chef profession in Ireland as part of my PhD research on this subject. In order to address this limitation, I undertook the first quantitative and qualitative gender inequality survey in the chef profession that permitted me to assess the stratification of roles and work environments in the Republic of Ireland. This chapter presents the results of this online chef survey *Step up to the Plate, Gender Inequality in the Chef Profession in Ireland*, which was undertaken between October 2016 and December 2016, confirming the

1 Mary Farrell, Farrell, Mary, 'Is it possible to uncover evidence of a gender revolution within food studies and professional culinary literature?' *Dublin Gastronomy Symposium* (2016) <http://arrow.dit.ie/dgs/2016/May31/16/>.

existence of, and nuances within, the gendered stratification of roles and work environments in the chef profession in Ireland. Further, comments within the survey highlight a gendered understanding of the profession that reinforces masculine and feminine stereotypes of chefs. I initially contextualize the chef profession, then briefly discuss the chef organizational model and the evolution of men and women's roles within it; I then discuss the methodology before presenting the qualitative and quantitative results of the chef roles and work environments in Ireland, followed by a discussion on the findings and nuances within the statistics.

Contextualizing gender within the chef profession

The 2016 Irish census statistics identify 23,732 chefs working in the hospitality industry in the Republic of Ireland, comprising of 31.1 per cent female chefs (Central Statistics Office 2016). This figure represents a proportional decrease in female representation of just over 2 per cent over the previous 2011 census data (Farrell 2018). Women represent less than one third of the Irish chef population, higher than in the United Kingdom, when 2017 statistics identified 23.5 per cent female chefs in the chef population, but lower than in the USA, as 2017 census data indicated 39.3 per cent of the chef population to be female (Bureau of Labor Statistics, 2017b; Office of National Statistics 2018). Research conducted in 2014 in Ireland found that only 14.5 per cent of *head chef* positions were occupied by females; again, this is higher than the United Kingdom figure of 18.5 per cent in 2016, but lower than female *head chef* representation in the USA, where in 2017 female *head chefs* represented 19.7 per cent of the *head chef* population (Allen and Mac Con Iomaire 2016; Bureau of Labor Statistics 2017a; Henderson 2017). Chef Danni Barry received a one star Michelin award in 2016 in Northern Ireland, one of only four women to receive this award on the island of Ireland following in the footsteps of Myrtle Allen (Michelin award 1975–80), Catherine Healy (Michelin award 1986–9), and Kai Pilz (Michelin award 1996–2001) (Mac Con

Iomaire 2018). Danni Barry and Jess Murphy won the Best Chef Award at the Restaurant Association Awards in 2017 and 2018 respectfully, the only two female chefs to do so since the Irish Restaurant Awards were first instituted in 2009 (Digby 2017, 2018).

These women stand out as exceptions in the culinary awards system, where men dominate overwhelmingly. These statistics reveal the under representation of women in the chef population overall and their very poor representation in leadership roles specifically. However, the data offers limited quantitative information to statistically assess gender inequality in chef roles, while no data exists on gender profile of chef work environments in Ireland. Before addressing the survey findings, the next section briefly outlines the organizational model that underpins the functioning of the professional kitchen, considering its impact on the gendered nature of the professional kitchen and its broader impact on society's understanding of chefs in the culinary world. While this system has evolved since its creation in nineteenth-century France, it remains the standard industrial organizational model used in many contemporary professional kitchens today.

The organizational model of the chef profession

The kitchen is the heart-beat of restaurants and food establishments, where professional chefs work within a clearly defined organizational structure to create, prepare and cook dishes to demanding and discerning customers in a variety of different food establishments. A key aspect of the professionalization of the chef profession was the introduction of the *brigade* system, an organizational structure introduced by Escoffier in the nineteenth century, to standardize work practice and ensure consistency of food production within the professional kitchen setting (Civitello 2008). The organizational model is based on the historical authoritarian hierarchical system, rooted in the military model where a chef's skill and status are understood by his/her role within the kitchen, revealing the long-established chain of command within this space (Fine Dining

Lovers 2016). The *head chef* or an *executive chef* sits at the top of the hierarchy, the leadership role in professional kitchens, typically in charge of directing others and providing creative leadership in recipe and menu development. Next in the hierarchy is the *sous chef*, or first line supervisor, who supervises workers in their various stations and prepares food, followed by the *chef de partie*, or line cook, who is in charge of a particular area of production such as fish section, meat section, cold and hot starter section and pastry. The *commis chef* or entry-level position role at the bottom of the hierarchy does food preparation work and basic cooking under the supervision of a *chef de partie* or section chef. Apprentice chefs work alongside *commis chefs* in the various sections preparing vegetables and ingredients for dishes in each section. The *pastry chef* is a highly skilled role, a *chef de partie* being skilled in making pastries, desserts, breads and other baked goods, and separate from the hot kitchen hierarchy often working independently in the kitchen. Depending on the size of the establishment and the economic imperative of success in an industry that operates within tight margins, many contemporary smaller restaurants operate a flat organizational model employing a smaller team of chefs. In this scenario a *head chef* may work with a *chef de partie* and/or *commis chefs*, apprentices and catering assistants. Large establishments and hotels employ a more extensive chef portfolio similar to the traditional hierarchical *brigade* model (Cullen 2012).

Stratification of roles

The evolving *brigade* organizational model remains relevant to understand the stratification of roles and women chefs' unequal status within the *brigade* system, where roles are defined along gendered lines within the professional kitchen. Historically, the 'ideal chef' as embodied by the *head chef*, is one of unquestioned authority, where loyalty, obedience, and strict discipline are demanded from staff, where strength, competitiveness, aggressiveness, and toughness are valued as ideal masculine traits within the kitchen environment, defined as hegemonic masculinity (Connell and

Messerschmidt 2005; Lane 2014). Connell and Messerschmidt (2005) argued that hegemonic masculinity plays an important role in legitimizing organizational power, typified by strong competent leaders. These qualities are generally associated with society's normative understanding of masculinity and represent the culturally idealized form of manhood that was socially and hierarchically exclusive, epitomizing the historically exclusive male chef profession. While younger, contemporary chefs are moving towards a more egalitarian civil interaction management model, research shows that discipline remains an integral part of fine-dining kitchens (Lane 2014). The chef profession tends to devalue qualities associated with our normative understanding of femininity: values of community, emotionality and caring where women chefs may be identified as 'invaders' because of their 'femininity' within the authoritarian historic *brigade* model (Harris and Giuffre 2015). As result, women are deemed to be lacking the necessary masculine qualities to lead a team of chefs in the role of head chef, while the pastry chef role is identified as a suitable feminine role, away from the serious masculine chef in the hot cooking section of the kitchen, thereby protecting the superiority of the masculine 'ideal chef'.

The gendered nature of chef roles is evident in wider social and cultural representations through media coverage of chefs and their restaurants. Analysis of print media, including restaurant reviews and chefs' profiles (2004–9) in USA revealed that chefs' roles were predominantly gendered, where *executive chef* roles were predominantly male and *pastry chef* roles were predominantly female (Harris and Giuffre 2015). Equally, this carries through in industry *via* chef competitions and awards when, in the USA, results of The James Beard Foundation annual culinary competitions in USA from 2009 to 2014 revealed that 67 per cent of the winners of the award for 'Outstanding Pastry Chef' were female (Forbes 2014). In no other category did women out-perform their male counterparts in these competitions, suggesting that the chef profession has evolved within its own unique organizational culture, where the identities of women and men appear to be shaped to create roles that are recognized as legitimate masculine and feminine roles within the profession. It is likely that the historically masculine hierarchical kitchen shaped the legitimatization of the *pastry chef* as a feminine role and the *head chef* roles as a masculine role within the masculine authoritarian *brigade* of this male dominated profession. Over time, this gendered understanding of roles became normalized within the profession, reinforced in contemporary society through media platforms and chef awards, thereby embedding the historically gendered roles as acceptable within contemporary culinary culture and in wider society. This is similar to the gendered division of labour in many occupations in European countries, with considerable variance at the national level (Catalyst, 2018; European Commission 2009). Television media representations of male chefs such as Gordon Ramsay in Hells' Kitchen reinforced this stereotypical image of an authoritarian masculine disciplinarian, while research of the television culinary programme Master Chef Australia found that this 'programme does little to challenge norms of the professional gastronomic field that have devalued women's cooking while valorising "hard" masculinized culinary cultures led by men'.[2]

Stratification of work environments

Chefs work in a variety of professional kitchens broadly categorized into two main areas, lower status day time service cafes, bakeries and industrial catering kitchens and higher status full-service (day and evening) restaurants that include casual dining, hotel and fine dining kitchens. Full-service restaurants operate for long hours, posing a particular challenge for women chefs who wish to have families or attend to their socially ascribed caring roles. Harris and Giuffre (2010) found that women chefs in Texas negotiate work–family conflict by using a variety of strategies that include choosing more family-friendly options like seeking work in establishments such as food production kitchens or cafes that operate day time working hours. Research in the UK highlighted female chefs tending to

2 Helen Herkes and Guy Redden, 'Misterchef? Cooks, Chefs and Gender in MasterChef Australia', *Open Cultural Studies* (2017), <https://www.degruyter.com/downloadpdf/j/culture.2017.1.issue-1/culture-2017-0012/culture-2017-0012.pdf>. 125.

work in day time professional kitchens, as opposed to their male counterparts, who make up the majority of chefs in the restaurant and hotel sector (Lutario 2010). Daytime work environments therefore offer women chefs the ability maintain a career in the chef profession, while also tending to their socially ascribed family duties and caring roles. While there are examples of women who have been successful despite the challenges, work–family conflict is recognized and well documented in research as a significant barrier within the hospitality industry, as within other organizations (Claringbould 2008; Walsh et al. 2014). It appears that chef work environments are also gendered, where women tend to work in lower status day time kitchens while men work in full-service higher status kitchens.

In order to assess the extent of the stratification of roles and work environments within the chef profession in Ireland, the next section first details the methodology, before presenting the results of the online chef survey *Step up to the Plate, Gender Inequality in the Chef Profession in Ireland* detailing the roles and work environments in which chefs work.

Methodology

The usable respondents within the survey was n = 475, consisting of 236 males and 239 females, a more or less even representation of both genders and comprising 2.13 per cent of the chef population. However, when comparing the observed frequency distribution of the variable 'gender' with its population distribution from the Central Statistics Office 2016 figures, there was a lack of representation with respect to this variable, as only 31.1 per cent of the chef population in Ireland was female. A weighing adjustment was performed on the variable 'gender' to reflect the gender representation in the national chef population.[3] Statistical testing was

3 The Central Statistics Office 2016 census statistics revealed that there were 16349 males and 7383 females in the chef population – females representing 31.1 per cent of the chef population (Central Statistics Office 2016).In order to ensure the survey

performed, and descriptive analysis carried out (frequencies and averages) along with inferential bivariate analysis (t-tests, Pearson's chi-squares of independence). The comments within the survey were manually analysed using thematic analysis (Braun and Clarke 2006s).

Analysis of the work environments revealed that almost 90 per cent of professional chefs worked in four key work environments: industrial catering,[4] casual dining, hotels and fine dining kitchens. The results of this sample (n = 432) are presented here with particular attention to the *head chef*, *pastry chef* and *commis chef* roles, to assess the extent of gender inequality in chef roles and work environments in Ireland.

Analysis

Analysis of comments within the survey identified stratification of roles as a highly significant theme for women chefs. They believed they were passed over for senior roles because of their gender or were stratified into a typically feminine *pastry chef* roles or into lower grade roles. Equally, there was an impression of a 'boys' club' mentality similar to the findings of Harris and Giuffre (2015), where women chefs were seen as 'invaders' and when male chefs treated them with a lack of respect, often using disparaging remarks towards their female counterparts. A female *head chef* (age 35–44) working in a 'hotel' kitchen, stated 'for female chefs, they have to be able for the banter and the boys' club of type of kitchen to get on, or they are just put in the pastry section just to make bread' or as one male *sous chef* (age 25–34) working in a 'hotel' kitchen remarked, 'I think there is a lot of discrimination in professional kitchens; I think there is a belief that women should be good at pastry cookery and are

data was reflective of the Central Statistics Office statistics, a weighted adjustment was then made using the auxiliary variable 'gender', ascribing a 1.388 weighting to male respondents and a 0.615 weighing to female respondents.

4 In this survey, industrial catering kitchen category included corporate catering, independent food production kitchens, hospital and school kitchens.

often just put in the pastry section of the kitchen at the start, think there is also lots of derogatory comments towards women'. The lack of female representation in senior roles was a major concern as a female *head chef* (age 45–54) working in an 'industrial catering' kitchen remarked, 'Not enough women making it to the top' and a female *pastry chef* (age 35–44) working in a 'hotel' commented, 'in all of the kitchens I have worked, women have been in the minority and I have only rarely seen a woman in more senior positions in kitchens'. This is further compounded by male chefs' lack of respect for females in senior positions as a female *pastry chef* (age 25–34) working in a 'hotel' kitchen outlines: 'males having issues taking direction from women'. These comments appear to indicate a gendered understanding of chef roles in many contemporary professional kitchens in Ireland.

In reply to the question in the survey 'do you think there is gender inequality in the chef profession in Ireland?' the majority, 57 per cent of female chefs in the weighted sample, agreed that gender inequality existed in the chef profession in Ireland while only 28 per cent of male chefs thought this was the case (Figure 1.1). Just over half of male chefs thought that gender inequality did not exist in the chef profession in Ireland.

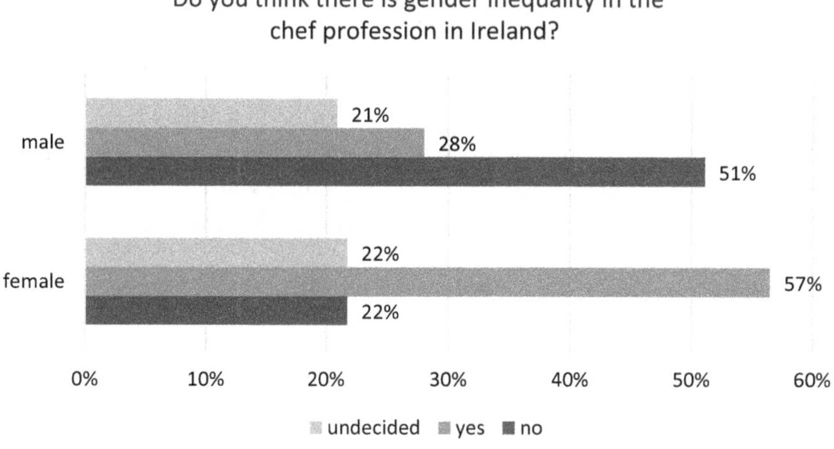

Figure 1.1: Gender inequality responses

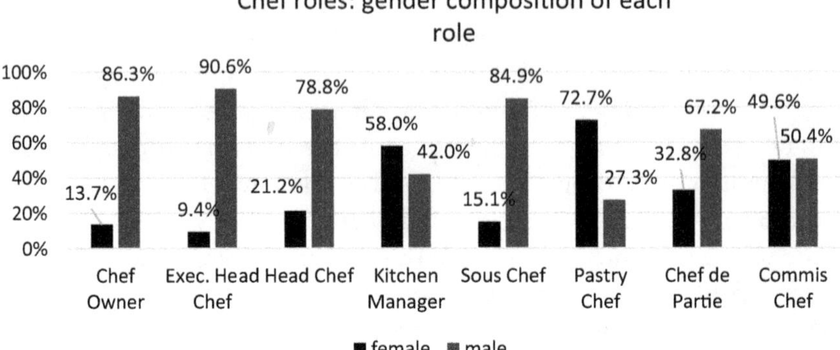

Figure 1.2: Chef roles: gender profile of each role

Analysis of chef roles in the four work environments identify a clear gender division in the distribution of chef roles in Ireland. Male chefs occupy the more senior roles: *executive head chef*, *head chef*, *sous chef* and to lesser extent, *chef de partie* roles. They also dominate the chef owner category, those chefs who own their own food restaurant or food establishment while also occupying the main chef role within this kitchen setting. Women are in the minority in all of the more senior categories, with the exception of kitchen manager. This role, while not included in the traditional chef hierarchy, is a senior leadership role in industrial food production kitchens, where the chef/manager leads a team of chefs and catering assistants and generally operates day time hours. Significantly, over 72 per cent of *pastry chefs* are women, the only chef role where women chefs overwhelmingly dominate, while women chefs are well represented at the *commis chef* level, possibly indicating female students' advancement in the culinary arts education in recent years (see Figure 1.2).

Head chef roles

The *head chef* role returned the most respondents in the survey (n = 82) and is the most common leadership role in the chef profession. Analysis of the weighted sample identified 21.2 per cent of all *head chef* roles in the four main work environments to be female, which is considerably higher than the finding of research conducted in 2014, which indicated a female *head chef* population of 14 per cent (Allen and Mac Con Iomaire, 2016). The female head chef representation of 21.2 per cent appears more in line with countries of similar cultural and economic backgrounds, as those of female head chef figures in United Kingdom (18.5 per cent in 2016) and USA (19.7 per cent in 2017) (Bureau of Labor Statistics, 2017a; Henderson 2017). This may indicate that accessing a broader and larger cross section of the chef population, and attributing a statistically representative weighting to gender in the methodology, offered a more accurate calculation of the gender composition of chef roles in Ireland.

Chi squared testing for independence was found to be significant for gender and work environments ($x^2 = 69.2$, df = 3, $p = 0.05$). When t-testing for significance of variance of gender (female: *mean* = 0.0530, *sd* = 0.0302; male: *mean* = 0.197, *sd* = 0.063) was conducted significance was identified, $t(6) = -4.089$ $p = 0.006$). *Head chef* roles are overwhelmingly dominated by men, where they occupy almost 79 per cent of these positions. The historically male dominated nature of the chef profession and their higher numerical presence and longevity in the industry can, to some extent, account for higher male representation here. However there is considerable variation in female *head chef* representation in each work environment. Almost 33 per cent of *head chef* population in industrial kitchens is female, reflecting very well on women's overall representation (31 per cent). This is supplemented by women's high representation in senior *kitchen manager* roles (58 per cent) in this work environment and builds on research, which found that women choose this work environment in order to attend to their socially ascribed caregiving roles. However the statistics indicate that *head chef* roles in full-service kitchens are not as accessible to women, with considerable variance evident within the three full-service kitchens. While women *head chef* positions in 'casual dining' work environments at 23 per cent is lower than their overall representation in the chef population (31.1 per cent), they are in an infinitely better position than their counterparts in the more elite 'hotel' and 'fine dining' work environment where female *head chef* representation is only 12.9 per cent and 13.7 per cent respectively, indicating a more favourable work environment for female chefs' progression in casual dining kitchens (Figure 1.3).

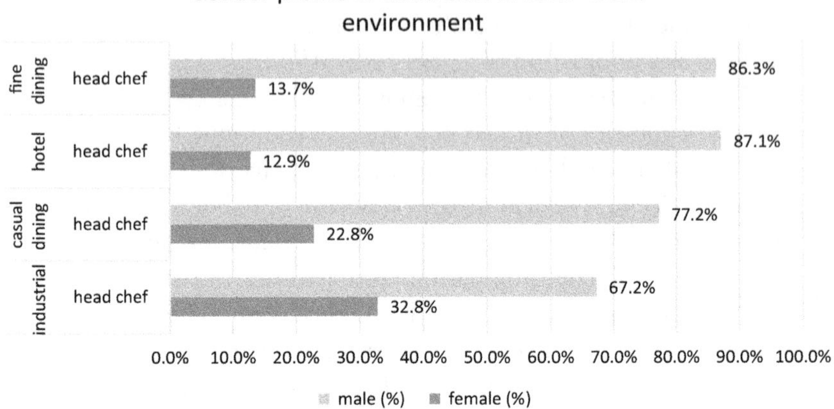

Figure 1.3: Gender profile of *head chef* role in each work environment

Pastry chef roles

Analysis of the sample sizes for *pastry chef* were small and the expected values fell below the required range for chi squared testing. Nevertheless, the data is useful to elucidate the gender composition of the *pastry chef* roles in the chef hierarchy in each of the work environments, in order to shed light on the extent of the gendered nature of the profession. The weighted sample of the *pastry chef* role is overwhelmingly dominated by females, with 72.7 per cent of being female, while only 27.3 per cent are male. This is the highest representation of females in any chef role by a considerable margin (Figure 1.2) This is the only role in which the majority of chefs in all work environments is occupied by females and strongly suggests that this is a gendered role within all work environments (Figure 1.4). This finding correlates with the findings in the literature, where this role is identified as a suitable 'feminine' role for female chefs and further research indicates that the *pastry chef* role is overwhelmingly a female role in each of the four work environments in the sample (Harris and Giuffre 2015).

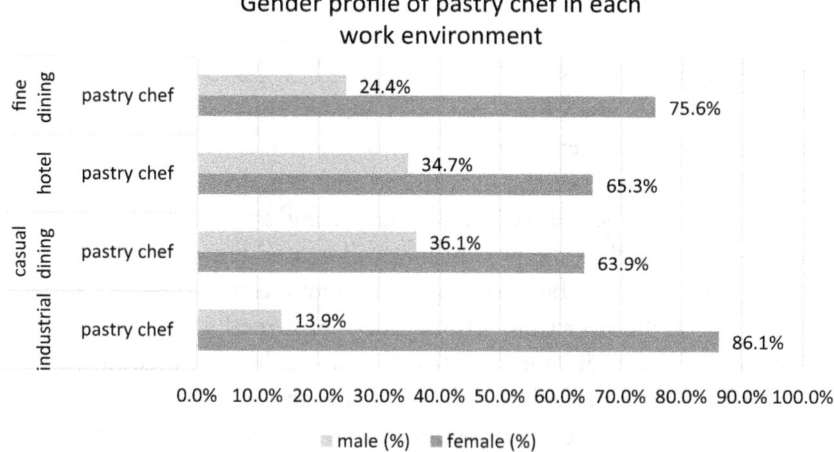

Figure 1.4: Gender profile of *pastry chef* in each work environment

Commis chef roles

The *commis chef*, the entry level chef role, identified a relatively even balance of male and female chef representation, at 50.4 per cent male and 49.6 per cent female (Figure 1.2). The gender breakdown was found to be significant when chi squared test of independence was conducted ($x^2 = 6$, df = 3, p = 0.004). No significance in variance of means (female: mean = 29.397, sd = 65.513; male: mean = 54.087, sd = 132.57) was found when t-testing was conducted ($t(6) = -0.03$, p = 0.975). Female chefs are very well represented in 'fine dining' and 'hotel' kitchen environments, much more so than any other role in the chef hierarchy, with the exception of *pastry chef*. Interestingly, female *commis chefs* are overwhelmingly found in 'casual dining' kitchens (Figure 1.5).

Analysis of longevity in the industry indicated that over 84 per cent of female *commis chefs* in 'casual dining' are new entrants in the '0–5 years' age category, indicating that females are entering this work environment in substantial numbers. This indicates that young female chefs are choosing to enter 'casual dining' kitchens in significant numbers and possibly see it as a viable career choice at the outset. It does appear that 'casual dining' work environment offers the best opportunity for female chefs to progress, when *head chef* roles are currently at 21.5 per cent and much higher than either of the other two full-service work environments. Nevertheless, analysis of the data found that female *commis chefs* in the '0–5 years' age category are entering 'fine dining' and 'hotel' work in high numbers, which offers the possibility of increased female representation in more senior roles in these work environments, as they progress through the chef hierarchy over time. This is only confirmed as they stay in this work environment, do not encounter, or are able to overcome barriers epitomized by the masculine culture of the *brigade* model as discussed here and highlighted by comments in this survey. Female *commis chef* representation was lowest in industrial kitchens at 22.8 per cent, even though women chefs are very well represented in the senior roles and in the pastry roles.

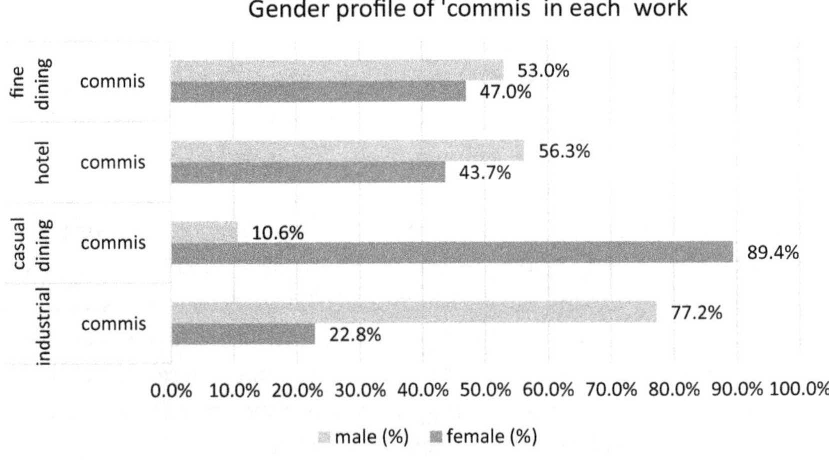

Figure 1.5: Gender profile of *commis chef* in each work environment

It is clear from the quantitative data presented here that while women are poorly represented in the more senior roles in the chef profession, there are considerable nuances within each of the four work environment categories. By contrast, the weighted survey results strongly suggest that the *pastry chef* is overwhelmingly a female role in Ireland, while women are very well represented in the lower grade *commis chef* roles in professional kitchens in Ireland. The next section discusses these results offering suggestions for the variations and nuances within the data that explain the challenges and possibilities for advancement of equality for women in the chef profession.

Discussion

The results of the survey confirm that *head chef* roles in professional kitchens in Ireland are the preserve of men, while also indicating considerable nuances within each of the work environments, where females are more highly represented in industrial catering and casual dining kitchens, compared to hotel and fine-dining kitchens. Previous research indicated that women chefs select day time service work environments that allow them to balance their professional life with their socially ascribed caring roles. The survey data builds on this research, indicating that industrial catering kitchens also offer a favourable career pathway for women chefs in Ireland, when the percentage of women chefs accessing head *chef* and *kitchen manager* positions is relative to, or higher than their overall statistical representation in the chef population in Ireland. This data suggests that a female-friendly work environment, where women are able to progress in stark contrast to *hotel and fine dining* kitchens, suggesting that the classic masculine authoritarian *brigade* model is less prevalent in the organizational stature. In addition, as women navigated to this work environment, their subsequent increased numerical representation possibly allowed them to draw on 'gender differences and as opposed to gender integration'[5] as a strategy to challenge stereotypes about femininity and

5 Deborah Harris, and Patti Giuffre, eds, '"Not one of the Guys", Women Chefs Redefining Gender in the Culinary Industry', *Gender and Sexuality in the Workplace, Research in the Sociology of Work* 20 (2010), 59.

women in managerial roles, similar to other professions (Britton, 2003; Williams 1989). Lower representation of female *commis chefs* in this work environment may indicate that women chefs currently start their careers in full-service kitchens and only navigate to industrial catering kitchens when family matters and caring roles arise, as research suggests. Alternatively, female chefs male encounter barriers relating to masculine culture within the *brigade* system of full-service kitchens and may choose to move to potentially more female-friendly industrial kitchens after some years.

The survey data indicates that female *head chef* representation is lower in all the three full-service work environments, with significant difference in representation in casual dining kitchens, when compared to both hotel and fine dining kitchens. Research suggests a lack of women in senior or leadership positions in all career choices, attributable to their lack of confidence in their own abilities, their negotiating skills (promotions, salaries), and their overall perception of themselves when compared to their male counterparts (Warrell 2016). Other research argues that an implicit stereotype threat is activated with subtle environmental cues, such as attributing negative descriptors to females in leadership roles or positions of power, resulting in women feeling conflicted about possessing this power or a lack of confidence in their abilities as a result of the negative descriptors of the implicit stereotype threat (Kelso and Brody 2014). However, higher levels of head *chef* and *kitchen manager* representation in industrial kitchens suggests that women are able to successfully overcome these barriers or that these specific work environments are more female-friendlier and supportive of women's advancement, as indicated above. Contrast this with very low female *head chef* representation in hotel and fine dining kitchens where the traditional *brigade* led kitchen is more prevalent and where barriers for women include masculinity, gender roles and expectation may account for low female *head chef* representation, as research suggests (Haddaji et al. 2017b). Women may therefore be considered unsuitable to run a professional kitchen that operates within the classic *brigade* system, 'the organization and its rituals are devalued if 'even a girl' can do them'.[6]

6 Dana Britton and Christine L. Williams, 'Don't Ask, Don't Tell, Don't Pursue: Military Policy and the Construction of Heterosexual Masculinity', *Journal of Homosexuality* 30/1 (1995), 15.

Elite kitchens such as 'fine dining' and 'hotel' kitchens are more male-dominated work environments and are more challenging for female chefs and these statistics appear to add further evidence that this is the case (Haddaji et al. 2017a). It may also be case that some casual restaurants in Ireland are moving away from the *brigade* model to a more egalitarian civil interaction management model, while also operating a flat organizational model where women chefs' career possibilities are enhanced and access to more senior roles increased in this work environment, as *head chef* statistics in casual dining kitchen in this survey indicate.

The quantitative statistics in the survey confirm the *pastry chef* role as a female role in all Irish professional kitchens, while comments within the survey suggest a gendered understanding of *pastry chef* roles within Irish professional kitchens based on the gendered assignment of roles in the masculine *brigade* hierarchical kitchen. However, the proliferation of the gendered understanding of the pastry chef role in all professional kitchens adds evidence to the normalization of this role within the culinary world and the impact of gendered representations on *pastry chef* roles through culinary awards systems and in broader cultural representations in society through media platforms. This in turn may legitimize the ascription of gendered roles by employers in professional kitchens, as part of the normal processes within the organizational structure of the masculine professional kitchen.

Female chefs are very well represented in the *commis chef* role in all full-service work environments, with a high proportion of them at the entry level. This is an encouraging finding and suggests that young females are viewing the chef profession as a positive career choice, not confined to the feminine pastry role. This appears to offers the possibility of increased female representation in more senior roles in full-service work environments over time, in particular in hotel and fine dining kitchens. It may appear to be exaggeration when I contend that female *commis chefs'* progression is dependent on a support work environment, a non-discriminatory work environment where young female *commis chefs* are recognized as equally capable and are given equal opportunity to work and progress in all sections in the professional kitchen on par with their male counterparts. The data from the survey indicates this to be a considerable challenge for women chefs, where it may be the case that these kitchens remain wedded to the masculine authoritarian hierarchy of the *brigade* organizational system which devalues women, their culinary skills and abilities because of their gender (Haddaji et al. 2017a).

Summary

To summarize, the results of the survey *Step up to the Plate, Gender Inequality in the Chef Profession in Ireland* confirm the gendered chef profession in Ireland, where chef roles and their work environments are stratified along gendered lines. Empirical data reveals that female chefs are poorly represented in senior *head chef* roles in all the three full-service work environments, but increasingly so in elite fine dining and hotel kitchens. In addition, the data from the survey suggests that casual dining kitchens may operate a less traditional masculine hierarchal *brigade* organizational model that may offer a more accessible career pathway to more senior roles, while the high numbers of new entrant female *commis chefs* offer the possibility of a change in gender profile of senior roles in all full-service work environments over time. This may be dependent on the dilution of the masculine *brigade* organizational set up to a more female-friendly, equal work environment. Conversely, lower status industrial catering kitchens offers a positive career pathway for female chefs while also reinforcing the gendered nature of the profession, as this work environment allows women to balance work, family life and caring roles. The *pastry chef* role is overwhelmingly occupied by female chefs in all work environments, substantiating research that it is a suitable feminine role in the masculine *brigade* organizational model of the professional kitchen. While women are making progress in the historically male dominated chef profession the empirical evidence indicates that many chef role and work environments remain stratified along gendered lines suggesting women chefs encounter considerable challenges in the chef profession in contemporary Ireland.

Bibliography

Allen, Hannah, and Mac Con Iomaire, Máirtín (2016). 'Against all odds: Head Chefs Profiled', *Journal of Culinary Science & Technology*, 14/2, 107–35.

Braun, Virginia, and Clarke, Victoria (2006). 'Using thematic analysis in psychology'. *Qualitative Research in Psychology*, 3/2, 77–01.

Britton, Dana (2003). *At work in the iron cage: the prison as gendered organization* (New York: New York University Press).

Britton, Dana, and Williams, Christine L. (1995). 'Don't Ask, Don't Tell, Don't Pursue: Military Policy and the Construction of Heterosexual Masculinity', *Journal of Homosexuality* 30/1, 1–21.

Bureau of Labor Statistics (2015). '11. Employed persons by detailed occupation, sex, race, and Hispanic or Latino ethnicity', <https://www.bls.gov/cps/cpsaat11.pdf>, accessed 27 November 2018.

—— (2017a). 'Food preparation and serving/chefs and head cooks', <https://www.bls.gov/ooh/food-preparation-and-serving/chefs-and-head-cooks.htm>, accessed 24 June 2018.

—— (2017b). 'Employed persons by detailed occupation, sex, race, and hispanic or latino ethnicity', <https://www.bls.gov/cps/cpsaat11.pdf>, accessed 27 March 2018.

Catalyst (2018). *Women in Male-Dominated Industries and Occupations*, <https://www.catalyst.org/knowledge/women-male-dominated-industries-and-occupations>, accessed 24 September 2018.

Central Statistics Office (2016). 'EB065: Population Aged 15 Years and Over, Employed Self-employed by Sex, Detailed Occupation and Census Year', <https://www.cso.ie/px/pxeirestat/Statire/SelectVarVal/Define.asp?maintable=EB065&PLanguage=0>, accessed 25 January 2019.

Civitello, Linda (2008). *Cuisine and Culture: A History of Food and People*, 2nd edn (Hoboken, NJ: John Wiley & Sons, Inc.).

Claringbould, Inge (2008). *Mind the Gap: The Layered Reconstruction of Gender in Sport Related Organizations* (Nieuwegein: Arko Sports Media).

Connell, Raewyn, and Messerschmidt, James (2005). 'Hegemonic Masculinity, Rethinking the Concept'. *Gender and Society*, 19/6, 829–59.

Cullen, Frank (2012). 'An Investigation in Culinary Life and Professional Identity in Practice during Internship', *Tourism Research Centre*, <https://arrow.dit.ie/cgi/viewcontent.cgi?article=1005&context=tfschcafoth>, accessed 21 January 2019.

Digby, Marie Claire (2017). 'Female chef named Best in Ireland', *The Irish Times* (9 May), <https://www.irishtimes.com/life-and-style/food-and-drink/female-chef-named-best-in-ireland-1.3075871>, accessed 21 February 2019.

'Dublin restaurant takes top spot at Irish Restaurant Awards' (2018). *The Irish Times* (15 May), <https://www.irishtimes.com/life-and-style/food-and-drink/dublin-restaurant-takes-top-spot-at-irish-restaurant-awards-1.3494984?>, accessed 2 January 2019.

European Commission (2009). 'Gender Segregation in the Labour Market, the root causes, implications and policy responses in the EU', <http://ec.europa.eu/commfrontoffice/publicopinion/archives/ebs/ebs_326_en.pdf>, accessed 23 November 2018.

Farrell, Mary (2016). 'Is it possible to uncover evidence of a gender revolution within food studies and professional culinary literature?' *Dublin Gastronomy Symposium* <http://arrow.dit.ie/dgs/2016/May31/16/>, accessed 21 January 2019.

—— (2018). 'Number of chefs rises by 25% in five years but more needed', *The Irish Times* (9 January, <https://www.irishtimes.com/life-and-style/people/number-of-chefs-rises-by-25-in-five-years-but-more-needed-1.3348785>, accessed 21 February 2019.

Fine Dining Lovers (2016). 'The Kitchen Family Tree', *Fine Dining Lovers*, <https://www.finedininglovers.com/blog/news-trends/food-infographic-kitchen-family-tree/>, accessed 23 January 2019.

Forbes, Paula (2014). 'By the Numbers: The James Beard Award Winners and Women', *Eater* (8 May), <http://www.eater.com/2014/5/8/6228723/by-the-numbers-the-james-beard-award-winners-and-women>, accessed 24 November 2018.

Haddaji, Madj, Albors-Garrigós, Jose, and García-Sigovia, Purificacion (2017a). 'Women Chefs' Access Barriers to Michelin Stars: A Case-Study Based Approach', *Journal of Culinary Science & Technology*, 15/4, 320–38, <https://doi.org/10.1080/15428052.2017.1289133>, accessed 1 February 2019.

—— (2017b). 'Women Professional Progress to Chef's Position: Results of an International Survey', *Journal of Culinary Science & Technology*, 16(3), 268–85. <https://www.tandfonline.com/doi/abs/10.1080/15428052.2017.1363109>, accessed 1 February 2019.

Harris, Deborah, and Giuffre, Patti, eds (2010). '"Not one of the Guys", Women Chefs Redefining Gender in the Culinary Industry'. *Gender and Sexuality in the Workplace, Research in the Sociology of Work* 20, 59–81.

—— (2015). *Taking the Heat, Women Chefs and Gender Inequality in the Professional Kitchen* (New Brunswick, NJ: Rutgers University Press).

Henderson, Emma (2017). 'The Women Proving Male and Female Chefs are Equal', *The Independent* (7 April), <https://www.independent.co.uk/life-style/food-and-drink/the-women-proving-male-and-female-chefs-are-equal-monica-galetti-a7660666.html>, accessed 3 January 2019.

Herkes, Helen, and Redden, Guy (2017). 'Misterchef? Cooks, Chefs and Gender in MasterChef Australia', *Open Cultural Studies*, <https://doi.org/10.1515/culture-2017-0012>, accessed 7 February 2019.

Gwendolyn, Kelso, and Brody, Lesley (2014). 'Implicit Processes and Emotions in Stereotype Threat about Women's Leadership', in Jin Zheng, ed., *Exploring Implicit Cognition: Learning, Memory and Social Cognitive Processes* (Hershey, PA: IGI Global), 118–37.

Lane, Christel (2014). *The Cultivation of Taste, Chef and the Organization of Fine Dining* (Oxford: Oxford University Press)

Lutario, Joe (2010). 'Survey Finds imbalance between male and female chefs', *Big Hospitality* (24 February), <http://www.bighospitality.co.uk/People/Survey-finds-imbalance-between-male-and-female-chefs>, accessed 24 January 2019.

Mac Con Iomaire, Máirtín (2018). 'A history of the Michelin Guide and Ireland', RTÉ, <https://www.rte.ie/eile/brainstorm/2018/1002/1000434-michelin-guide-stars-ireland/>, accessed 21 January 2019.

Office for National Statistics (2018). 'Office for National Statistics, April–June 2017, United Kingdom', <https://www.ons.gov.uk/employmentandlabourmarket/peopleinwork/employmentandemployeetypes/datasets/employmentbyoccupationemp04>, accessed 27 February 2018.

Walsh, Kate, Fleming, S., and Enz, Kathy (2014). 'Female executives in hospitality: Reflections on career journeys and reaching the top', *Cornell Hospitality Reports*, <https://scholarship.sha.cornell.edu/chrpubs/161/>, accessed 21 December 2018.

Warrell, Margie (2016). 'For Women To Rise We Must Close "The Confidence Gap"'. *Forbes* (20 January), <https://www.forbes.com/sites/margiewarrell/2016/01/20/gender-confidence-gap/#13595ef81efa>, accessed 24 February 2019.

Williams, Christine (1989). *Gender at work: Men and Women in Non-Traditional Occupations* (Berkeley: University of California Press).

YVONNE MURPHY

2 Sexual consent: Are the lines really that blurred?

Sex without consent is rape. While this should be a straightforward concept for individuals to understand, research seems to suggest otherwise (Humphreys 2007). The recent and explosive occurrence of the #MeToo movement on an international scale also proposes that, anecdotally, the sexual harassment and assault of women is rampant in almost every industry imaginable.[1] Ireland is no exception in terms of industry[2] and its own movements.[3] With high-profile men disputing accusations of alleged sexual harassment, assault or inappropriate behaviour as 'locker room talk'[4] or 'banter',[5] this chapter contends that while it has never

1 In their 2018 study Fitzgerald and Cortina condensed numerous studies highlighting the industries and areas where women and girls have been subjected to sexual harassment: 'workplaces and universities, by strangers in public, by landlords in their homes and apartments, by teachers and peers in high schools, and even in middle schools, nurses are harassed by physicians and female physicians by patients, service workers by customers, hotel maids by guests and female inmates by correctional officers' (2018: 215).

2 'A total of 46 women (2.9 per cent) and 40 men (2.6 per cent) of the SAVI sample indicated that they experienced at least one form of sexual harassment by someone within their work environment' (McGee et al. 2002: 165). 11 per cent of the women who took part in the USI Say Something report responded that they had been subject to unwanted sexual contact in University (USI, 2013).

3 #IBelieveHer: this hashtag and subsequent demonstrations were a direct response to the verdict of The Belfast Rape Trial and in solidarity and support of survivors of sexual violence and the woman at the centre of the trial (#IBelieveHer, 2018).

4 Donald Trump Apology, 10 October 2016: 'This was locker room talk. I am not proud of it. I apologise to my family, I apologise to the American people. Certainly, I am not proud of it. But this is locker room talk' (NBC NEWS, 2016).

5 Belfast Rape Trial: *The Irish Times* reported that 'All three accused said they were embarrassed by the texts they sent, explaining them variously as "exaggeration", "nonsense" and "banter"' (Gallagher, 2018).

been acceptable to harass or assault a woman, at present, women's views on sexual subjectivity[6] and sexual consent are changing (Satinsky and Jozkowski 2015). Satinsky and Jozkowski (2015) found that features of sexual subjectivity are essential in allowing adult women communicate their wants and needs in sexual situations. Consequently, women's boundaries are also shifting.

The purpose of this chapter is to demonstrate that sexual consent is a concept that evolves for individuals as they age, not only in terms of comprehension but also through the progression of language. Participants reported having a better understanding of sexual consent at their current age compared with their teenage years. The theory of liminality will be utilized in order to support the understanding of this evolution. Liminality focuses on rites of passage (Parker, Ashencaen Crabtree, bin Baba, Paul Carlo and Azman 2012) or what Turner (cited by Bigger, 2010) referred to as being 'betwixt and between' (2010). It is also argued that rather than sexual consent being a concept that has to evolve in meaning for people, it should in fact be approached in an entirely different fashion. A case for applying a feminist postmodern framework will be presented and an argument will be made that traditional views of sex, consent and sexual violence should no longer be considered 'women's issues'. Using qualitative research methods, the results of interviews with eight women regarding their relationship with sexual consent and the manner in which it changes over time will be analysed.

All of the women interviewed for this research were living in Ireland at the time of interview. Not all of the women were originally from Ireland, three of them were born in other parts of Europe but all had been living and working in Ireland for the last number of years. In order to asses if participants views of sexual consent evolved over time, a requirement for taking part in the research was that everyone had to be over 25 years of age. The age of participants ranged from 26 to 62 and the relationship status of the women varied from single, polyamorous, in a relationship, married, married with children and widowed.

6 'Sexual subjectivity is conceptualized as becoming the subject rather than the object of desire' (Satinsky and Jozkowski, 2015: 414).

Additionally, this chapter will demonstrate that older people[7] are undervalued and overlooked as a resource. Existing research predominantly focuses on younger people and their present views on sexual consent, suggesting obvious gaps in research. Furthermore, it will highlight that the opportunity to learn more from if or how an individual's understanding of consent evolves overtime is not being utilized. This research has been influenced by a number of feminist scholars and their work on sexual consent. The work of Pineau, Beres and Powell along with other prominent researchers in the area will be unpacked and examined to better understand consent as a concept and in practice.

Traditional sexual script

It would not be possible to adequately understand the concept of sexual consent without first examining the traditional sexual script. Sexuality was first linked to social scripting by Gagnon and Simon in 1973, after they had observed comparisons between actors following scripts on stage with how people engage in sexual activity (Wiedreman 2005). Beres, Herold and Maitland (2004) argue that script theory has been helpful for researchers in trying to understand behaviours around consent and has been used considerably when researching sexual activity and communication. They explain that the sexual script is largely based on the assumption that people recognize the sexual situations they may find themselves in and have a shared understanding of how to behave in said situations (Beres et al. 2004). Wiederman posits that sexual scripts, in Western society, are completely different for men and women (2005), this point has been echoed by a series of researchers. In their study, Jozkowski and Peterson (2013) found that participants had very distinct views when it

7 The age range of women in this study was 26 to 62 years of age. None of the participants were in college at the time of the interview. The ages broken down: two in their twenties, two in their thirties, two in their forties, one in their fifties and one in their sixties.

came to gender and sexual activity. Men were viewed as those who should initiate sexual activity, leaving women to take up the role as sexual 'gate keeper'. They also found the theme of men's pleasure being seen as more important within the sexual experience, thus leaving the woman's enjoyment as secondary (2013). Humphreys (2007: 309) assessment is similar as he argues that traditionally women 'have been socialised to play a defensive role in sexual situations'. This research has identified a moving away from the acceptance of traditional sexual scripts and a heteronormative view of consent.

Defining sexual consent

Remarkably, research on the topic of sexual consent has been limited (Jozkowski and Peterson 2013; Humphreys 2007; Humphreys and Herold 2007) and at present there is not one fixed, agreed upon definition of sexual consent applied by scholars. Jozkowski and Peterson (2013: 517) found that some researchers have come up with 'self-generated definitions of consent'. While Beres (2014) asserts that the concept of consent is regularly taken for granted by researchers as they assume a shared understanding of it, without actually defining it. In an earlier study Beres (2007) gives a number of examples where scholars neither define nor review literature on consent, leading to the assumption that all readers have a shared understanding of consent. Beres describes this as 'spontaneous consent' (2007: 97).

Beres (2007: 97) does concede that there seems to be a general consensus among scholars that sexual consent signifies some form of 'agreement to engage in sexual activity'. However, this is where consensus ends as there is some disagreement with regards to the conditions under which agreement happens (Beres 2007). There is the 'any yes' approach which is potentially problematic, as this view could result in a yes that is acquired through force or coercion being deemed consensual (Beres 2007: 97). Other scholars, Beres (2007) argues, view consent as something which needs to be voluntary or freely given and must include willingness to take part in sexual activity. In their 2018 study on the sustainability and feasibility of consent workshops in third-level institutions in Ireland, MacNeela, O'Higgins, McIvor, Seery, Dawson, and Delaney used the definition of sexual consent embraced by Muehlenhard and Hickman (1999: 259, Beres, 2007), which defines consent as 'the freely given verbal or nonverbal communication of a feeling of willingness to engage in sexual activity' (2018: 3). In her later research when Beres interviewed participants regarding the manner in which they negotiated sexual activity, along with their definitions of sexual consent, she found they described consent in three key ways; consent as a minimum requirement,[8] as a discrete event[9] and as something that does not apply to their relationships (2014).

Conversely, Pineau has arguably the most comprehensive view of sexual consent, what she referred to as the communicative model. The communicative model is a mix of having an awareness of your partner and an understanding of desire (1989). Pineau likens this model to holding a decent conversation,[10] it is usually easy to tell when people are interested in a topic of conversation verses people who seem disinterested, distracted or give one word answers (1989). Engaging in consensual sexual activity, Pinuea believes, should hold the same principles as a good conversation. Thus if using the communicative model became the norm, it would be easy for people to tell if their partner does not wish to engage in sexual activity. Therefore, if sexual activity were still to occur it would be due to either 'reckless disregard or willful ignorance' and consequently should only be defined as rape (1989: 239). Moreover, if there was a communicative

8 For the majority of respondents this was the absence of no and something that was almost considered a legal requirement (Beres, 2014).

9 Discrete event: agreeing to go home with someone or what some referred to as a '*buttlift*', when a woman manoeuvres her body in such a way that her partner is able to remove her underwear (Beres, 2014: 383)

10 Good conversationalists do not shout or get angry or loud with their peers, they are empathetic and wait for natural breaks in conversation rather than overwhelm the other person with their views. They are interested in what the other person thinks and feels and if the conversation does become aggressive or reaches an impasse the conversation will usually come to a close, as people are not expected to sit quietly while being berated by another (Pineau, 1989).

approach to sexuality then there would, in theory, no longer be the sexual 'miscommunications' (Powell, 2010: 87) that could lead to non-consensual sex (rape) or sexual violence. In addition, consent would become something that was more explicit and easy to identify (Beres, 2007) and would take responsibility for proving non-consensual sex took place away from the victim and put it squarely on the perpetrator to prove that consent had been obtained (Beres, 2007).

Token resistance

Token resistance is another theme that is frequently mentioned in research on sexual consent, partly due to its proximity to the traditional sexual script. Muehlenhard and Peterson describe token resistance as 'indicating to a partner that one does not want to have sex when in fact one does' (2005: 15) or what Powell referred to as sexual 'miscommunications' (Powell, 2010: 87). Humphreys and Herold argue that token resistance can have a negative impact on the manner in which consent is negotiated (2007). It can lead to potentially dangerous miscommunications such as men questioning if a woman's objection to sexual activity is indeed genuine (Jozkowski and Peterson, 2013). This also puts women into a contradictory situation where they have to put across that they are sexually interested in a potential partner while not coming across as too available so as not to be perceived as being 'easy' (Wiederman, 2005; Muehlenhard, Humphreys, Jozkowski, and Peterson, 2016).

Additionally, the belief in token resistance arguably suggests that the 'just say no' approach to consent can have dangerous implications for women (Burkett and Hamilton, 2012: 817), if their no is not adhered to. They go on to argue that this approach is one of 'risk avoidance' which again puts the burden on women to keep themselves safe (2012: 817). Interestingly, when Muehlenhard and Peterson asked participants in one of their studies to elaborate on instances of token resistance they had experienced, respondents ended up describing what Muehlenhard and Peterson started referring to as the discourse of ambivalence (2005).

Discourse of ambivalence

Instead of individuals discussing instances of token resistance, Muehlenhard and Peterson found that respondents were actually describing ambivalence around wanting and not wanting sex (2005). This led them to change their initial model of simply looking at sex as being dichotomous, that is, wanted or unwanted, and open it up to become something more complex. This new model, the 'missing discourse of ambivalence' (2015: 15), allowed for 'multiple dimensions' (2005: 17) when it came to sex such as differentiating between wanting just sexual activity and wanting its results. This model also crucially includes space for differentiating between being coerced into having sex, wanting to have sex and actually consenting to it. They argue that there are many reasons in which people can consent to sexual activity without actually wanting it (2005). Muehlenhard and Peterson argue that adopting this framework may be helpful when investigating women's sexuality in future, as well as being beneficial if implemented into classroom settings to help young people recognize and share their feelings around sex (2005).

Feminist postmodern framework

The methodological approach taken by this research is a feminist one. Miner-Rubino, Jayaratne, and Konik provide a good overview of what exactly it means to employ a feminist methodology by contending that the research carried out should be based on feminist principles along with a vision for social change (2007). More specifically, this research has adopted a feminist postmodern framework. Hesse-Biber emphasizes the attraction many feminists have to postmodernism is that it highlights the 'other' within the research process (2007: 12). She continues by linking postmodernism's significance with empowering oppressed groups with that of feminisms goal of social change and justice (2007). Feminist postmodernism emphasizes the need for practising a feminism that is truly intersectional.[11]

Hesse-Biber acknowledges that some have argued a downside of feminist postmodernism being that it can destabilize feminist theory as it challenges binary categories such as women and gender, which has resulted in the polarization of feminist theory (2007). The purpose of this research is to give women of various ages, who are traditionally left out of these conversations, a voice and most importantly, to move away from sexual violence and traditional views of sex and consent being considered 'women's issues'. Letherby contends that 'Feminist Postmodernism does not try to resolve the problems of other positions; rather it starts from a different place and proceeds in other directions' (2003: 51). This chapter will demonstrate that perhaps by taking a feminist postmodern approach to consent and sexual violence where it is no longer just a 'women's issue' but a societal issue, could arguably lead us to a place of new discourse and redefined and positive engagement.

The method chosen for this research was qualitative, specifically in the form of interviews. Perhaps one of the first and most influential advocates for the qualitative method was Oakley. Oakley (cited by Letherby, 2003) stressed the importance of letting women share their experiences through developing a 'participatory model' of using in-depth interviews. This was viewed as one of the most effective ways to examine how people live, along with being morally responsible (2003: 85). Additionally, Beres states that moving towards a qualitative approach to consent can result in findings that 'present a more complex picture of sexual consent' (2007: 105).

11 Kimberlé Crenshaw first introduced intersectionality, where she recognized the manner in which oppression can affect people in many different ways and on more than one level (1989). For example, women of colour face more oppression than white women because they have to contend with racism as well as sexism.

Interviews were conducted one-on-one and were semi-structural in nature. There were no strict criteria in place for participants, the only stipulation was that each individual had to live in Ireland and be over the age of 25. This was deliberate in order to understand if participant's views of consent had changed or evolved from when they were teenagers to their current age. All other participant demographics were left wide open, this was also intentional as sexual violence can affect anyone.[12] The intention was to amplify the voices and opinions of women who are reflective of what contemporary Ireland looks like today.

The sampling strategy employed was snowball sampling;[13] this was due to the subject of sexual consent potentially being sensitive in nature for some people to discuss, along with a possible reluctance to initially engage on the subject. Although snowball sampling can have limitations in terms of variety of participants, in this case the decision was made that the safety, comfort and welfare of all participants took priority. All interviews began with participants reading an article on the cancelation of sexual consent workshops in University of Limerick due to lack of interest.[14] This was to elicit initial conversation on the topic of consent in a natural and relaxed manner, as the wellbeing of all participants was of the utmost importance. Their ages ranged from 26 to 62, one woman identified as queer, the rest as heterosexual, three women were not originally from Ireland but all were residents of Ireland.

DeVault and Gross argue that feminist researchers are all too aware of the damage done by previous waves of male-centric research that misrepresented women's experiences, and as such hold themselves to a higher ethical standard (2007). The wellbeing and privacy of participants in this

12 In the 2002 SAVI report over 3,000 Irish adults were randomly selected to take part, participants varied in age, gender, education levels, marital and work status. 42 per cent of women and 28 per cent of men 'reported some form of sexual abuse or assault in their lifetime' (McGee et al. 2002: xxxiii).

13 Snowball sampling: 'A technique for finding research subjects. One subject gives the researcher the name of another subject, who in turn provides the name of a third, and so on' (Vogt, 1999).

14 University of Limerick forced to cancel sexual consent workshops over lack of interest, 2 March 2017, found at: <http://www.thejournal.ie/sexual-consent-ul-3266632-Mar2017/> (Murray, 2017).

research was paramount; all names have been changed, and at no point were participants asked about their previous sexual experiences, this was also made clear before interviews took place. Some participants did speak briefly about previous sexual experiences; however, they were reminded they did not have to do so and were asked repeatedly if they wished to continue and how they were feeling. Noble and Smith outline strategies that researchers can adopt to ensure the validity and reliability of their qualitative findings such as 'including rich and thick verbatim descriptions of participants' accounts to support findings' (2015: 34–5). When analysing interviews and highlighting common themes, precise quotes from participants will be applied in this research. This process is referred to as thematic analysis.

Findings

The initial definitions of sexual consent provided by participants were quite similar, however, as the concept was unpacked they began to appear noticeably different in some cases. These findings are similar to that of Coy, Kelly, Elvines, Garner and Kanyeredzi who found when interviewing teenagers on the topic of consent all participants had a clear understanding of consent in abstract terms, but this began to shift when being applied to real-life situations (2013). The approaches to consent offered by participants mirrored those found by previous researchers in their studies.

Consent as a mutual agreement

MARY: [smiling] I think it has to be both people, am, (short pause) wanting to do what they're doing. That's it really.

INTERVIEWER: Mm.

MARY: And be present and aware of what is being done.

CAROL: Okay, so, consent is both parties agreeing to engage in a sexual act. That's the way that I would look at it that you need to have both individuals wanting to (short pause). Yeah, that there's a yes from both parties to engage in a sexual act.

When asked to define sexual consent everybody initially gave clear and similar responses showing that they all had a firm grasp of the concept in abstract terms. The most popular approach included the mutual agreement of both parties. This view would match closest with consent being defined as a mutual willingness and agreement between partners to engage in sexual activity (Beres, 2007; Hickman and Muehlenhard, 1999).

Consent as a minimum requirement

ANNE: I suppose like if it's a one night stand, you would need to kinda get some kind or form of consent, obviously not 'are you sure you want to do this?'

One participant's initial definition of consent equated with the minimum requirement or any yes approach to sex as being sufficient (Beres, 2007; 2104). This approach is not as robust as the former as arguably even if the yes was obtained through coercion or force it could still be considered consent (Beres, 2007).

Consent as a discrete event

SARAH: I felt because I brought him home, (short pause) and even though I had asked him to stop I was still like, well like, I was up for it initially.

There was the view of consent being communicated through a discrete event, such as going home with someone (Beres, 2014). While this understanding was not overtly stated by an actual participant, it was implied that the participant's partner possessed this comprehension, and as a result led to what the participant referred to as an ambiguous situation or what could also be considered as a 'miscommunication'.

Sexual miscommunication theory

> SARAH: I suppose in my own head there was ambiguity there about, am, difficulty I felt because I brought him home (short pause) and even though I had asked him to stop I was still like, well like, I was up for it initially and then like, I changed my mind, so I suppose he was probably like 'well you wanted it, like you brought me home'.

This miscommunication and feeling of responsibility could be due to sexual miscommunication. Sexual miscommunication results in the onus of communicating the refusal of sex being put squarely on women (Beres, 2010; Powell, 2010). The theory proposes that miscommunications between men and women can lead to instances of heterosexual sexual violence or coercion. The specific miscommunications are believing women engage in token resistance and women's enthusiasm in sex being over estimated by men (Beres, 2010). Beres argues that some researchers are also guilty of assuming that consent is gendered in nature, meaning women give consent to men (2007), this can potentially lead to the reproduction of problematic views of consent. For example, if a woman is perceived to be engaging in token resistance then her 'no' may not be taken seriously (Jozkowski and Peterson, 2013). Participants also gave examples of potential sexual pressure they have faced:

> BARBARA: I know that in hindsight, retrospectively looking back on some situations they definitely weren't consensual.

ANNE: I know once or twice there may have been situations that, if I knew about consent and you didn't really have to regardless, now nothing serious, don't get me wrong but like, there are situations I regret getting into and being in.

MARY: Maybe when I was younger I could have been persuaded to try things that maybe I had not wanted to do.

At no point did any of the women put responsibility for stopping the activity on their partners, it was not even considered, and they all exhibited self-blame. Interestingly, sexual miscommunication was the only reference to any sort of obvious gendered themes with regards to consent and responsibility. Despite a strong presence of the traditional sexual script (Wiedreman, 2005; Beres et al. 2004) and token resistance (Muehlenhard and Peterson: 2005) being prevalent in the majority of earlier studies on consent, those themes were not as apparent in this study, even with it regularly being depicted in popular culture (Jozkowski and Peterson, 2013).

Liminality and the evolution of consent

Analysis shows that for the majority of participants sexual consent was undeniably a concept that has evolved in meaning for them over time. This evolution will be broken down into views participants had when they were teenagers and their current definition of consent. The concept of liminality will be employed to explain the dramatic shift in individual's views.

Liminality is focused on rites of passage and when people transition from one social positioning to another (Parker et al. 2012). Arguably such liminal states include moving from teenage years and the transition into adulthood. Thematic analysis illustrates that participants changing views from their teens to the present day demonstrates how moving through this liminal stage and becoming an adult resulted in them being able to better define sexual consent. Many participants admitted to feelings of fear and inexperience at a young age being partly responsible for this evolution, while others stated ignorance or ambivalence about the topic. Conversely, all but one of the participants expressed being more confident and knowledgeable in terms of sex and consent at their current age. The themes that emerged suggested that participants in their younger years were evolving through a liminal stage from adolescence into adulthood and as a result they had not yet grasped an adequate definition of consent.

Younger years

Many participants felt they did not have a good handle on what consent meant in their younger years. This caused them to fall into situations without realizing they had a choice, leading some to believe that they were at fault. Powell highlights the after-effects that experiences of not being able to negotiate sexual encounters assertively can have on women, by stating that it can lead to low self-confidence (2010). While Satinsky and Jozkowski (2015, citing Tomlan) believe that 'developing a sense of oneself as a sexual subject is necessary for an individual to make active sexual choices that meet one's needs for both sexual pleasure and sexual safety' (2015: 414).

Nancy referred to herself as being very naive in her beliefs about consent as a teen, she had an idealist view of how her life would play out:

> NANCY: I was very clear when I was like 16 or 17 that, ah, like, the world was safe and perfect.

Helen and Barbara admitted to consent not being on their radar, with Helen going on to say that she did not get any sort of helpful information from either school or at home and this left her figuring it out for herself:

> HELEN: I don't remember there being one thing about consent or even in school I don't remember there being one thing. Aam, it could

> have been really helpful, especially when you were a teenager, I don't know whether I would have gone, but it might have been in there somewhere, do you know? [laughs]
>
> INTERVIEWER: Yeah.
>
> HELEN: Sooner than me figuring it all out for myself, I don't know.
>
> BARBARA: I don't think I would have been that aware of (short pause) the whole concept of consent in the way that it's framed now.

Being critical of the type of sexual education in schools available to participants was a strong theme, with other participants mentioning their sexual education was either lacking or non-existent:

> MARY: It was just pretty much biological.
>
> CAROL: I didn't get any exceptional sex education at school either.

The manner in which consent was largely ignored within their sexual education leaving them figuring things out for themselves is conceivably quite problematic. McKee, Albury, Dunne, Grieshaber, Hartley, Lumby and Mathews assert that young people need to be taught about consent, not just in terms of themselves but also with regards to other people (2010). Powell concurs by stating that there is a need for sexual education that is progressive and inclusive (2010).

Current age

All of the participants, apart from one, feel they are more vocal, knowledgeable and confident in sexual situations now than they were in their younger years. Currently they have a clear picture of what consent means to them. Arguably, it was going through the liminal stage from adolescence to adulthood and becoming more self-aware and mature that brought this new found confidence:

> ANNE: You know? I'm more mature now and I'm older and I'm like, 'dude, really? No'.

Satinsky and Jozkowski assert that women become more self-assured communicating consent when they feel more entitled to their sexual pleasure (2015: 424).

For Nancy it was also coming to terms with recognizing and being responsible for her feelings and not being afraid to name and share them:

> NANCY: I remember really, like a light bulb going off and saying, and I was 25 or 26, saying I'm in my 20s I am responsible for telling people how I feel.

McKee et al. maintain that it is essential for young people to be educated around treating people in an ethical manner, especially in relationships (2010).

Some participants believe that consent today needs to be approached in a different way. Barbara thinks that not only should we put more trust in young people when teaching them about sex, we should make it more applicable to real life and make it okay for someone to say that they are not sure what sexual consent is about:

> BARBARA: I don't know how many people would admit to like, in a situation, 'oh I don't really understand consent.' So maybe like making it okay to (short pause) want to know about it or something maybe?

Powell found that when asking young people to make suggestions about the kind of sexual education they wanted they suggested more 'real-life' discussion including scenarios that were likely to happen and the skills needed to deal with them (2010: 135). Young people wanting to learn more and be informed about sex suggests a maturing and liminal move into the responsibility of adulthood.

Society is also slowly beginning to evolve, people no longer believe in old wives tales[15] and laws protecting people from sexual violence are starting to improve. Last year (2017) is the first time that Ireland has seen a legal definition of sexual consent written into law.[16]

Evolving consent

As previously highlighted, despite the abundance of research in areas around sexual violence, research into consent is still rather limited (Beres, Herold, and Maitland, 2004; Humphreys and Herold, 2007; Jozkowski and Peterson, 2013). Moreover, it is not just in relation to consent where noted gaps in research lie, McKee et al. (2010, citing Lagerberg) assert that the sexual development of young people has not yet been entirely explored or understood (2010). There also appears to be a gap in research on the possible evolution of consent. The closest was a study by Coy et al. where they found a comparable, yet unexplored theme of evolving consent. They stated that older teenagers had a better grasp of conditions that legally constituted rape and as a result advocated for the consideration that teenagers understanding of consent may change over time (2013). Arguably, what the researchers are referring to here is the concept of liminality.

15 TARA: 'I mean I remember a friend of mine when she first started having sex with her boyfriend, she told me, and I said to her be careful, and she told me you can't get pregnant the first time. Which she did, of course.'

16 'A person consents to a sexual act if he or she freely and voluntarily agrees to engage in that act' (Criminal Law Sexual Offences Act 2017 Section 48).

The importance and progression of language

Sociolinguists suggest that language could be considered a reflection of society (Hawkins, 2013 citing Grimshaw). This makes the language used by participants when speaking about sexual violence and consent particularly interesting. Many participants alluded to acts of sexual violence when they were speaking but they did not say the actual words. However, a theme that was present was a separate language of inclusion. The manner in which individuals initially defined consent is worth noting as it was free of gender binaries and assumptions about sexual orientation. This also suggests a possible progression or evolution in how participants view consent, as individuals move away from the traditional sexual script and heteronormative explanations of the concept.

A common theme throughout the majority of the interviews conducted was the absence, avoidance or hesitation to say words associated with sexual violence. Both Anne and Nancy refer to sexual violence as 'stuff'. When speaking about an ad campaign depicting sexual violence Helen made reference to 'the violence' and Barbara spoke of the need for clarity with consent in reference to 'a courtroom situation'. Each participant was obviously referring to rape or sexual violence yet none of them said the words. In the interview with Mary on the first occasion she mentioned the word rape she paused twice before saying it, however, after her initial pause she did go on to use the word 'rape' a number of other times throughout the interview.

Kelly advocates for feminist activists to pay more attention to language that is used by women in order to better aid with defining abusive or violent experiences, as similarly in her study she found that women had difficulty naming instances of sexual violence (1988). Another example is when Sarah referred to an incident where her consent was not given but the partner in question attempted to continue with the act. At no point did she name what happened as a violation, she also refrained from using the word 'sex':

> SARAH: I was up for it initially and then like, I changed my mind, so I suppose he was probably like 'well you wanted it, like you brought me home'.

Additionally, this incident contains signs of victim blaming.[17]

Although language can be used as an oppressive tool, it can also be utilized in the fight against patriarchal influence (Letherby, 2003) allowing for more inclusive language and as such move away from exclusory discourse. While the majority of previous research on consent has included strong themes of heteronormativity, exclusion of the LGBTQ+ community and use of the traditional sexual script, this research appears to be moving away from such strong heteronormative narratives. The initial definition of consent given by every participant made no reference to gender binaries or orientation. Although some participants did go on to speak in binary terms, there were numerous instances of inclusive language being used, along with acknowledgement of same sex couples and how little conversations about consent are framed around them:

> ANNE: You'd get a feeling for how things are progressing between you and the guy or girl.
>
> MARY: You just shouldn't be doing things to another person regardless of their gender or regardless of your gender.
>
> BARBARA: I definitely think though that in terms of same sex couples, it's probably, or couples or people, I suppose, and their interactions with consent is probably something that we don't hear about too much either.

Surprisingly, there was much less mention of the traditional sexual script than expected, given its prevalence in previous research (Wiedreman, 2005; Beres, Herold and Maitland, 2004). Carol made reference to men being 'more sexually driven' and that they 'kind of listen to that sexual drive'. While Helen made reference to the script on a larger scale, 'I think the whole culture of, I guess, women should be pliable and say yes and men are on the attack kind of thing' observing that this belief is a cultural and problematic one.

Conversely, while many of the participants did not make an overt reference to the traditional sexual script, it does appear that certain

17 Victim blaming is a process that occurs almost exclusively in cases of sexual violence where often the female victim is blamed or in some way held responsible for their assault (Grubb and Turner, 2012).

beliefs regarding sexual responsibility may have been internalized by some participants, this has been addressed through the aforementioned belief in and reference to sexual miscommunication (Beres, 2007). Though this theory is not as apparent as the traditional sexual script it could potentially be seen as a moving away from viewing consent and sexual activity in obvious binary and heteronormative terms. However, it should be noted that much work still needs to be done to be more inclusive of members of the LGBTQ+ community, including those who identify as trans, queer and/or non-binary. Weinberg argues that people consciously using inclusive language can help promote self-acceptance with those in the LGBT community (2009). This use of inclusive language and move away from strong themes of the traditional sexual script suggests that perhaps the concept of sexual consent is also evolving within society.

Recommendations for future education and policy development

The main findings of this study suggest that the manner in which the majority of individuals define consent is indeed nuanced and complex. What has also been established by this research is that individuals understanding of consent is something that has unquestionably evolved for them over time and the concept of liminality has been used to aid in the understanding of this. Consequently, these findings have given risen to a potentially notable result with regards to how sexual consent could be approached going forward. This new framework could arguably result in younger generations not having to go through the same unnecessary evolution in their relationship with sexual consent.

The language and themes conveyed by participants reaffirmed the using of a feminist postmodern lens through the moving away from overtly gendered social scripts within their views of consent. However, as previously discussed other problematic albeit less obvious gendered beliefs were held by numerous participants, namely the sexual miscommunication theory. This theory and the finding here suggests that concerning gendered assumptions of sex and consent still exist in some form. Powell believes that it is possible for young people to be (knowingly or unknowingly) complicit in reproducing these gendered assumptions and their negative results (2010: 71). Though arguably, a positive aspect of this new framework is that it could lead us to move away from unhelpful approaches to sexual violence prevention that likely results in forms of victim blaming (Burkett and Hamilton, 2012). The use of this approach was also influenced by Powell and her inspiration taken from Foucault and his concept of agency through reflexivity and discourse (2010).

While there is no denying that men are predominantly the perpetrators of violence against women (WHO, 2016) and this should be recognized, the current framing of violence against women being a 'women's issue' is problematic. Although Chapleau (2015, citing Baynard) found there has been a recent shift in sexual violence prevention campaigns broadening to suggest that it is also a men's problem (2015), there needs to be further progression within this movement. The current framing of violence against women and indeed consent assumes that the burden of responsibility to stay safe is on women (Beres, 2010; Powell, 2010; and Burkett and Hamilton 2012). Additionally, this view can leave men feeling vilified that they are continuously portrayed as perpetrators of violence (McElroy, 2014) and as a result can leave them reluctant to get involved in any form of discourse on the matter. This polarization of the genders does nothing but stall the conversation on consent and sexual violence prevention. Powell has also argued that the same gendered rhetoric on sexuality and consent has been in place for forty years; namely women's sexual passivity and gendered double standards (2010; Coy et al. 2013). She goes on to say that part of the reason for the confusion and complexity young people have in negotiating sex and consent is due to 'embodied gendered practices' (2010: 86–7; Coy et al. 2013). Until now the majority of research on sexual consent has been heteronormative, Lafrance, Loe and Brown have even referred to discussions of 'hook-up' culture as being 'heterosexist' (2012: 445). Perhaps an answer to this problem is a new approach to sexual consent free from gender binaries. Arguably, this research is evidence that it is possible for society to move away from viewing sexual consent and sexual violence in terms of binaries or women's issues, due to participants demonstrating their move away from use of the traditional sexual script and the inclusive language they used, as their views of consent and sex evolved over time.

If people are looked upon as mere individuals and not defined by their gender or orientation, and a framework with regards to sex and consent similar to Pineau's communicative sexuality (1989) was adopted, along with the inclusion of a discourse of ambivalence (Muehlenhard and Peterson, 2005), everybody would arguably be on the same playing field. Pineau posits that this model not only takes the responsibility of refusing consent off of women but instead relocates responsibility to the other party to prove that consent was actually obtained (1989; Beres, 2007). This approach is similar to that of affirmative consent[18] (Muehlenhard et al. 2016) though debatably much less regimented. In their recent study on rape supportive beliefs Klement, Sagarin and Lee found that members of the BDSM[19] community, who have long-standing practices of affirmative consent, reported remarkably lower levels of belief in rape myth acceptance, victim blaming and benevolent sexism (2017: 133).[20] While the results of that particular study were promising, it appears there are other groups within society that may not want such a regulated version of sexual consent.

When Antioch College in Ohio mandated a comparable sexual consent policy[21] in 1996 the outcomes of studies on it were not as favourable. Humphreys and Herold explored what students in different

18 Affirmative consent suggests that consent is a conscious, obvious and voluntary agreement to engage in sex that continues throughout the entire activity. Not only can it be revoked at any stage but silence, and/or the absence of resisting or protesting does not imply consent (Muehlenhard, Humphreys, Jozkowski, and Peterson, 2016).

19 BDSM: bondage/discipline, dominance/submission, sadomasochism (Beres and McDonald, 2015: 418).

20 Benevolent sexism 'is characterized by the attitude that women who are traditionally feminine should be rewarded' (Grubb and Turner, 2013: 447).

21 'The Sexual Offense Prevention Policy (SOPP) is a campus wide policy of Antioch College. All sexual interactions at Antioch College must be consensual. Consent

colleges thought of this policy. They found that the majority of students were not in favour of it, believing it to be extreme, unrealistic and too difficult to enforce. Respondents feared the policy could make the sexual activity awkward and robotic, and essentially less pleasurable (2003). Therefore, the use of communicative sexuality is potentially a better framework. Not only for reasons already stated but additionally, if practised correctly there is no need for explicit and ongoing verbal consent throughout the sexual activity (Beres, 2007; Pineau 1989) thus making it more natural and less mechanical. Communicative sexuality promotes that sexual activity include morality, good communication and mutual enjoyment (Pineau, 1989). Finally, it is being argued that the adoption of this approach could prevent any more 'sexual miscommunications' from occurring (Powell, 2010: 87).

Furthermore, adding the discourse of ambivalence to this framework could go on to allow people to comprehend the complexities between wanted, unwanted, consensual and coercive sex (Muehlenhard and Peterson, 2005). It could also open up the discourse to allow people explore their feelings around sex and consent as there is more involved in sexual activity than just a simple dichotomy of sex being either wanted or unwanted (Muehlenhard and Peterson, 2005). This in turn could result in providing individuals with the strategies and skills to refuse sex in a confident manner, along with the understanding and awareness to know when consent is not being given.

Consequently, broadening and reframing our approach to consent could result in responsibility falling on everyone, thus make it everyone's issue inclusively, not just a gendered one. This could potentially result in the eradication of the practice or belief in rape myths and victim blaming to some degree. In theory, it could lead to perpetrators of sexual violence being the ostracized minority within society and not the victims, and it would give people space to question their feelings and actions with regard to sexual activity including working through a lack of understanding on the concept of consent.

---

means verbally asking and verbally giving or denying consent for all levels of sexual behavior. Non-consensual sexual behavior, verbal and physical sexual harassment are not tolerated at Antioch College' (Antioch College, 2016).

Conclusion

Aside from a consideration made in a 2013 report (Coy et al.) there appears to be a gap in literature regarding the evolution of sexual consent, as well as using the perspectives of older people on this subject. Exploring this strand of consent did however, provoke an unforeseen result by presenting possible new ways in which society could approach consent. Beres (2007, citing Pineau) surmised that we need to change how we think about consent and engaging in sexual activity (2007) and the proposal provided arguably does just that, providing a model that would fit well both in Ireland and internationally. Recommendations for further research would be to continue investigating how and why individuals views of sexual consent changes over time and the manner in which this could inform policy and aid in our teaching of sexual education going forward.

In one manner this study has echoed what has been found in previous research that at present there is no one general consensus or agreed upon definition of sexual consent. Therefore, the answer to the overarching research question is; when it comes to sexual consent, it appears the lines really are that blurred.

Bibliography

Antioch College (2016). *The Antioch College sexual offense prevention policy*. Yellow Springs, Ohio: Antioch College. Available: <http://www.antiochcollege.edu/sites/default/files/04.015_Sexual-Offense-Prevention-Policy.pdf>, accessed 30 August 2018.

Bigger, S. (2010). *Thresholds, Liminality and Fruitful Chaos: Revolutionary Change in Education?*, Worcester Research and Publications, available: <http://eprints.worc.ac.uk/834/1/Turner_article_Submitted.pdf>, 1–13, accessed 17 August 2018.

Beres, M. A. (2007). '"Spontaneous" sexual consent: An analysis of sexual consent literature', *Feminism & Psychology*, 17(1), 93–108.

—— (2014). 'Rethinking the concept of consent for anti-sexual violence activism and education', *Feminism & Psychology*, 24(3), 373–89.

——, Herold, E. S., and Maitland, S. B. (2004). 'Sexual Consent Behaviors in Same-Sex Relationships', *Archives of Sexual Behavior*, 33(5), 475–86.

——, and McDonald, J. E. C. (2015). 'Talking about Sexual Consent: Heterosexual Women and BDSM', *Australian Feminist Studies*, 30(86), 418–32.

Burkett, M., and Hamilton, K. (2012). 'Postfeminist Sexual Agency: Young Women's Negotiations of Sexual Consent', *Sexualities*, 15(7), 815–83.

Chapleau, K. M. (2015). 'Using Masculinity to Stop Sexual Violence: Must Women Be Weak for Men to Be Strong?', *Sex Roles*, 73, 86–9.

Coy, M., Kelly, L., Elvines, F., Garner, M., and Kanyeredzi, A. (2013). '*Sex without consent, I suppose that is rape': How young people in England understand sexual consent*, A report commissioned for the Office of the Children's Commissioner's Inquiry into Child Sexual Exploitation in Gangs and Groups, available: <http://cwasu.org/wp-content/uploads/2016/07/CONSENT-REPORT-EXEC-SUM.pdf>, accessed 17 August 2018.

Crenshaw, K. (1989). 'Demarginalizing the Intersection of Race and Sex: A Black Feminist Critique of Antidiscrimination Doctrine, Feminist Theory and Antiracist Politics', University of Chicago Legal Forum, 1989(8), 139–167 available: <http://chicagounbound.uchicago.edu/uclf/vol1989/iss1/8>, accessed 17 August 2018.

DeVault, M. L., and Gross, G. (2007). 'Feminist Interviewing: Experience, Talk, and Knowledge', in Hesse-Biber, S. N., ed., *Handbook of Feminist Research Theory and Praxis*, pp. 173–198.

Ehrlich, S., and King, R. (1998). 'Gender-Based Language Reform and the Social Construction of Meaning', in Cameron, D., ed., *The Feminist Critique of Language:* A Reader, London: Routledge, pp. 164–79.

Fitzgerald, L. F., and Cortina, L. M. (2018). 'Sexual harassment in work organizations: A view from the 21st century'. In C. B. Travis, J. W. White, A. Rutherford, W. S. Williams, S. L. Cook, and K. F. Wyche (eds), *APA handbooks in psychology series. APA handbook of the psychology of women: Perspectives on women's private and public lives*, Washington, DC: American Psychological Association, pp. 215–34.

Gallagher, C. (2018). 'Three accused in rape trial say texts were "exaggeration" and "banter"', *The Irish Times*, 10 March, available: <https://www.irishtimes.com/news/crime-and-law/three-accused-in-rape-trial-say-texts-were-exaggeration-and-banter-1.3421575>, accessed 30 August 2018.

Grubb, A., and Turner, E. (2012). 'Attribution of blame in rape cases: A review of the impact of rape myth acceptance, gender role conformity and substance use on victim blaming', *Aggression and Violent Behavior*, 17, 443–52.

Hawkins, G. M. (2013). *Language and the Social: Investigations Towards a New Sociology of Language*, unpublished thesis (PhD), London School of Economic and Political Sciences, available: <http://etheses.lse.ac.uk/690/1/Hawkins_Language_and_the_social.pdf>, accessed 17 August 2018.

Hesse-Biber, S. N. (2007). 'Feminist Research: Exploring the Interconnections of Epistemology, Methodology, and Method', in Hesse-Biber, S. N., ed., *Handbook of Feminist Research Theory and Praxis*. London: Sage Publications, pp. 1–28.

Hickman, S. E., and Muehlenhard, C. L. (1999). '"By the semi-mystical appearance of a condom": How young women and men communicate sexual consent in heterosexual situations'. *Journal of Sex Research*, 36, 258–72.

Humphreys, T. (2007). 'Perceptions of Sexual Consent: The Impact of Relationship History and Gender', *The Journal of Sex Research*, 44(4), 307–15.

——, and Herold, E. (2003). 'Should Universities and Colleges Mandate Sexual Behaviour?', *Journal of Psychology & Human Sexuality*, 15(1), 35–51.

——, and Herold, E. (2007). 'Sexual Consent in Heterosexual Relationships: Development of a New Measure', *Sex Roles*, 57, 305–15.

Jayaratne, T. E., and Stewart, A. J. (2008). 'Quantitative and Qualitative Methods in the Social Sciences: Current Feminist Issues and Practical Strategies', in Jagger, A. M., ed., *Just Methods: An Interdisciplinary Feminist Reader*. London: Paradigm Publishers, 44–57.

Jozkowski, K. N., and Peterson, Z. D. (2013). 'College Students and Sexual Consent: Unique Insights', *The Journal of Sex Research*, 50(6), 517–23.

Kelly, L. (1988). *Surviving Sexual Violence*. Cambridge: Polity Press.

Kleinman, S. (2007). *Feminist Fieldwork Analysis: Qualitative Research Methods Series 51*, Los Angeles, CA: Sage Publications.

Lafrance, D. E., Loe, M., and Brown, S. C. (2012). '"Yes Means Yes": A New Approach to Sexual Assault Prevention and Positive Sexuality Promotion', *American Journal of Sexuality Education*, 7, 445–60.

Letherby, G. (2003) *Feminist Research in Theory and Practice*. Buckingham: Open University Press.

McElroy, M. (2014). 'The big lie of "rape culture"', The Future of Freedom Foundation, available: <http://www.fff.org/explore-freedom/article/the-big-lie-of-a-rape-culture/>, accessed 17 August 2018.

McGee, H., Garavan, R., deBarra, M., Byrne, J., and Conroy, R. (2002). *The SAVI Report. Sexual Abuse and Violence in Ireland. A national study of Irish experiences, beliefs and attitudes concerning sexual violence.* Dublin: Liffey Press.

McKee, A., Albury, K., Dunne, M., Grieshaber, S., Hartley, J., Lumby, C., and Mathews, B. (2010). 'Healthy Sexual Development: A Multidisciplinary Framework for Research', *International Journal of Sexual Health*, 22(1), 14–19.

MacNeela, P., O'Higgins, S., McIvor, C., Seery, C., Dawson, K., and Delaney, N. (2018). *Are Consent Workshops Sustainable and Feasible in Third Level Institutions? Evidence from Implementing and Extending the SMART Consent Workshop*. Galway: School of Psychology, NUI Galway.

The Irish Examiner, '#IBelieveHer rallies taking place nationwide in aftermath of Belfast rape trial', 29 March 2018, available: <https://www.irishexaminer.com/breakingnews/ireland/ibelieveher-rallies-taking-place-nationwide-in-aftermath-of-belfast-rape-trial-834804.html>, accessed 2 September 2018.

Miner-Rubino, K., Jayaratne, T. E., and Konik, J. (2007). 'Using Survey Research as a Quantitative Method for Feminist Social Change', in Hesse-Biber, S. N., ed., *Handbook of Feminist Research Theory and Praxis*. London: Sage Publications, pp. 199–222.

Muehlenhard, C. L., Humphreys, T., Jozkowski, K.N, and Peterson, Z. D. (2016). 'The Complexities of Sexual Consent Among College Students: A Conceptual and Empirical Review', *The Journal of Sex Research*, 53(4–5), 457–87.

——, and Peterson, Z. D. (2005). 'Wanting and Not Wanting Sex: The Missing Discourse of Ambivalence', *Feminism and Psychology*, 15(1), 15–20.

Murray, S. (2017). 'University of Limerick forced to cancel sexual consent workshops over lack of interest', The Journal.ie, 2 March, available: <http://www.thejournal.ie/sexual-consent-ul-3266632-Mar2017/>, accessed 30 August 2018.

NBC News (2016), 'Donald Trump On 2005 Tape: "This Was Locker Room Talk"', *NBC News* [video], available: <https://www.youtube.com/watch?v=IEOOoMjhVsU>, accessed 30 August 2018.

Noble, H., and Smith, J. (2015). 'Issues of validity and reliability in qualitative research', *Evidence-Based Nursing*, 18(2), 34–5.

Parker, J., Ashencaen Crabtree, S., bin Baba, I., Paul Carlo, D, and Azman, A. (2012). 'Liminality and learning: international placements as a rite of passage', *Asia Pacific Journal of Social Work and Development*, 22(3), 146–58.

Powell, A. (2010). *Sex, Power and Consent: Youth Culture and the Unwritten Rules*. Cambridge: Cambridge University Press.

Satinsky, S., and Jozkowski, K. N. (2015). 'Female Sexual Subjectivity and Verbal Consent to Receiving Oral Sex', *Journal of Sex & Marital Therapy*. 41(4), 413–26.

Union of Students Ireland (2013). *Say Something: A Study of Students' Experiences of Harassment, Stalking, Violence & Sexual Assault*. Dublin: Union of Students Ireland.

Violence against women Intimate partner and sexual violence against women Fact sheet (2016) World Health Organization, available: <http://www.who.int/en/news-room/fact-sheets/detail/violence-against-women>, accessed 17 August 2018.

Vogt, W. P. (1999). *Dictionary of Statistics and Methodology: A Nontechnical Guide for the Social Sciences*. London: Sage.
Wiederman, M. W. (2005). 'The Gendered Nature of Sexual Scripts', *The Family Journal: Counselling and Therapy for Couples and Families*, 13(4), 496–502.

CELIA DE FRÉINE

3 The woman who would teach Irish

Louise Gavan Duffy was born in Cimiez near Nice in 1884, the second child of the third family of Charles Gavan Duffy and his wife, Marie Louise née Hall. Marie Louise was 28 years of age at the time, forty years her husband's junior. Before Louise had reached the age of 5, her mother was dead. She and her older brother, George, and younger brothers, Bryan and Thomas, were raised from then on by their half-sisters Susan, Harriet and Geraldine. Louise's childhood and early education in France were to have a lasting effect on her and to influence the educational work she would later accomplish in Ireland.

Her father, Charles Gavan Duffy, statesman, patriot, poet, historian, journalist and member of the Young Ireland Movement, was co-founder and editor of *The Nation*, one of the first newspapers in Ireland written in English that was aimed at cultivating a sense of nationalism among the native Irish. After a significant career in Ireland as journalist and Member of Parliament in Westminster, Gavan Duffy emigrated to Australia in 1856 where he carved out a political career during the twenty-three years that followed.

Gavan Duffy had suffered from respiratory problems since his youth and by 1880, when his eyesight had begun to fail, he decided to retire to the French Riviera. At this time the temperate climate of Nice and its environs attracted many invalids. No cure could be found for their ill-health but the good weather added to their life expectancy. Gavan Duffy settled in Cimiez at first and subsequently moved to Nice.

Nice was a city where everyone spoke at least two languages. As well as French, the natives spoke Niçard, a patois which comprised a mixture of dialects related to those of Liguria in Italy and Provence in France. French was the compulsory language for school children who, from 1882, under the Jules Ferry Law, were obliged to attend school between the ages of 6 and 13. Not only was French compulsory in the classroom, it was the only language permitted in the school yard.

Louise later recalled her schooldays:

> My brothers and I went to school with French children, played with French children and were very happy among them – but we were intensely conscious of our nationality and determined to leave no one that we met, even the most passing acquaintance, in ignorance of the fact that we were Irish. (Gavan Duffy, 1966)

> At times Louise's classmates would ask: 'Why do you speak English among yourselves?' – and we [she and her brothers] were too ignorant to give them the true answer. (Gavan Duffy, 1966)

Although convinced of her nationality, the question as to why her family spoke English at home would intrigue the young girl in years to come. Unknown to her, Irish, the language of her forebears, was still spoken in the *Gaeltacht* [Irish-speaking areas] on Ireland's western seaboard and, as a result of the concerted efforts of *Conradh na Gaeilge* [the Gaelic League], was being revived in towns and cities.

The use of English had become widespread during the Famine years when would-be emigrants realized it was the language that would enable them to find work in England or America: 'roughly half the population could speak Irish prior to 1845, only about 14 percent could in 1901' (MacDonagh, 1983, 104). Other circumstances had contributed to the demise of Irish during the first half of the eighteenth century also. In 1831, the Stanley Letter put paid to the poor schools that had succeeded the hedge schools, and introduced a system that required all subjects be taught through English in school. This new system, coupled with the disrespect the Catholic Church had for Irish aided its decline.

During his tenure as editor of *The Nation* (1842–1852), Charles Gavan Duffy, had been dismissive of the Irish language and had contributed, in no small part, to the spread of English. *The Nation* had a wide appeal in that it drew on Irish tales, promoted Irish nationalism and recounted Irish history, but was written in English. According to Leon Ó Broin, one of his biographers, Gavan Duffy used the familiar rhythms and cadences of Irish when composing verse and ballads for publication in the newspaper:

> He did not know any Irish but he realised that the translations of the songs he had heard in his youth were an element that linked the Irish people with their past and that could be used to animate their political ambitions. (Ó Broin, 1967, 10)

Gavan Duffy was not the only Young Irelander who held little regard for Irish:

> His attitude to the Irish language was that of the Young Irelanders generally. In the first year *The Nation* printed at least two articles on the Irish language. They were by Davis, who, with John Pigot, earnestly wished for a wider extension of the use of Irish ... Duffy was constrained by Davis to use the Irish form of place-names ... in the text of The Nation's ballads and he protested to MacNevin that they were going too far. (Ó Broin, 1967, 145–46)

MacNevin was of the opinion: 'We must be cosmopolitan ... and deviate occasionally from our native bogs.' Ó Broin's understanding of this comment is that: 'Irish ... was thus a mere bog language and a badge of serfdom while Ireland's survival lay through the employment of English' (Ó Broin, 1967, 146). He develops this thought in the case of Gavan Duffy's attitude to the language as follows: 'Duffy personally behaved as if Irish did not exist and certainly felt no obligation to ensure its survival' (Ó Broin, 1967, 147).

Although unaware of the existence of the Irish language, Louise and her brothers were familiar with Irish history and lore. 'We were of course brought up in the tradition of 48 and gathered some knowledge of history and current events in Ireland from the conversation of our elders and from the many Irish visitors coming to the house' (Gavan Duffy, 1966). Among these visitors were John Dillon, Dora Sigerson and Douglas Hyde, co-founder of *Conradh na Gaeilge*.

Louise and her brothers were sometimes privy to these conversations but would at times draw the wrong conclusion or make their own of what they had overheard. According to Ó Broin: 'Louise ... remembers the constant talk about Parnell and Gladstone whom, in her innocence, she conceived as two gladiators confronting each other in a large hall supported by gangs of noisy partisans' (Ó Broin, 1967, 143).

In 1983, when Louise was 9 years old, Douglas Hyde visited the Gavan Duffy household in Nice, while on honeymoon with his bride, Lucy Kurtz.

Hyde had an interesting conversation with Gavan Duffy in the latter's library, which he recounts in his memoir *Mise agus an Connradh* [Myself and the League]:

> He was a great story-teller and he told me that he loved stories when he was young ... and that he was always urging his mother to tell him another. And in the end she would say: 'Oh, darling ... I couldn't tell you another story unless I told it to you in Irish.' That was enough. It never occurred to his mother that she ought to speak Irish to him and tell him stories in Irish. And it probably never occurred to him either, until that day I was talking to him ... He said to me again 'that if anyone had told him that time, when he was in Ireland, that four people would come together in any one room to practise Irish, I would not have believed it. (De h-Íde, 1937, 27–8; all translations from Irish to English in this essay by Celia de Fréine)

What is clear from this conversation is that while Gavan Duffy might not have shared Hyde's belief in Irish, what the honeymooner said, cast doubts on Gavan Duffy's attitude to it: if someone as erudite and well-educated as Hyde believed in the revival of Irish, then perhaps there was some worth in the language, after all.

Louise was not, however, present during this conversation. Gavan Duffy was a typical Victorian father who saw his children only briefly during the day. Louise was 15 years of age before she discovered the existence of the Irish language, old enough to engage her father in conversation. By this time he was 83 years of age, almost blind, ensconced in his library trying to commit to paper what he knew of Irish history and his involvement in it.

One day, while perusing a list of books, she discovered that:

> the Irish had their own language. I well remember the occasion as I was very taken by it. It happened that I was examining a list of old books, that came to the house one day, when I saw the words *A grammar of the Irish language for sale*. This statement so surprised me that I immediately ran to my father to find out what it meant. My eyes opened wide when he told me that Irish was still spoken in places in the country and that his mother was an Irish speaker, even though she did not teach him the language. I made myself a promise that day that I would learn Irish and, when one of my brothers managed to locate a couple of the Ó Gramhna [*sic*] booklets some time afterwards, I set about the work with devotion. But I didn't get on so well, over in France, without a teacher. (Gavan Duffy, 1966)

Not only was Gavan Duffy's mother a native speaker of Irish but, as the books indicate, Irish was still being spoken in Ireland. It was Louise's older brother, George, who had become articled to a firm of solicitors in London, who brought home to her the grammar books in question. It was from these that she began to teach herself Irish. There were five books in the series written by Ó Gramhnaigh and published by *Conradh na Gaeilge*. Sales of these books were phenomenal and by 1903: 'the League had published more than 320,000 copies of the first volume of the series alone' (McMahon, 2008, 10).

As Gavan Duffy neared the end of his life he continued to write and to correspond with his many friends. His autobiography *My Life in Two Hemispheres* was published in 1898. According to Ó Broin:

> He was practically blind and had to rely on his daughters and on Father John Fitzpatrick, an Oblate friend, to read to him and to write his letters. The reading lasted four or five hours a day because, apart from the newspapers, he loved stories – in particular, those of Scott, Thackery and Conan Doyle. Essays and poetry he enjoyed too. Edgar Allan Poe was a favourite of his ... This reading chore was rather hard on the daughters; but it probably never occurred to Duffy that he was being inconsiderate; in those days it was not 'the done thing' for young women to go out to work; so that some useful employment had to be found for them at home. After all, girls were only girls. (Ó Broin, 1967, 151)

At that time second- and third-level education were unavailable to most girls in Ireland and France and there were few career opportunities for women in either country. However, during Gavan Duffy's tenure as editor of *The Nation*, several women contributed regularly to the newspaper. Such writing was, however, looked on as a pastime or as auxiliary work. If the women in question did not have a legacy to provide them with enough to live on, they had fathers or husbands to support them.

As her father's health deteriorated Louise would go for a walk with him every morning. Although the children had been in awe of him when young, he encouraged them to talk to him as they grew older. It is interesting to speculate on what topics of conversation Louise and her father engaged in during these walks; there can be little doubt, however, that Louise shared with him her keen interest in the subject closest to her heart, that of Irish.

When her father died in 1903 Louise was among the mourners who accompanied his body to Ireland, setting foot on her native soil for the first time. She was overwhelmed by the number of people who, anxious to pay their respects to the last of the Young Irelanders, turned out for his funeral. Much had changed in Ireland in the realms of education, culture and language during the years since her father's departure.

As a result of the Intermediate Education (Ireland), 1878 Act and the University Education (Ireland), Act, 1879, which established the Royal University, Catholic men could attend university. From 1882 on the Royal University could confer degrees 'ar mhic léinn a rinne staidéar ar a gconlán féin nó a d'fhreastail ar fhorais oideachais fheiliúnacha' [on students who studied on their own or who attended recognized educational foundations] (Ó Glaisne, 1991, 272). *Coláiste Naomh Muire* [St Mary's College], a university college founded by the Dominican nuns and attended by Catholic women, was one such college.

The Irish Women's Suffrage and Local Government Association, founded in 1876, was the first of many organizations which would seek the right of women to vote. Some women who were involved in these organizations believed that the vote should be sought first; others believed that the independence of the country should be achieved first and that then, all other civic rights, including the right of women to vote, would follow.

Demand for literary, cultural and sporting organizations was met by the Pan-Celtic Society, the National Literary Society, the Irish National Theatre Society and the Gaelic Athletic Association, all of which were founded between 1888 and 1898. Political organizations such as *Inghinidhe na hÉireann* [Daughters of Ireland] and *Cumann na nGael* [Society of Irish People] were both founded in 1900. Sinn Féin [We Ourselves], one of the first political parties to allow women equal membership, was founded in 1905.

Conradh na Gaeilge, founded in 1893 by Douglas Hyde and others, was going from strength to strength. Louise had read about this organization, studied two of the Ó Gramhnaigh books and had 'dúil dóite aice teanga a tíre féin a fhoghlaim [a burning desire to learn her own country's language]' (Luccan, 1993, 8). While in Dublin, she availed of the opportunity to visit the *Conradh* offices. It was here she discovered the widespread, varied and propagandist work the organization engaged in:

> It was not until some years later that, coming to Ireland for the first time for my father's funeral ... I saw the language written and heard it spoken by an old man who received me, when I called at the Gaelic League office. (Gavan Duffy, 1966)

Louise later confided to Nóra Luccan: 'dar léi féin, b'in í an uair ar chuir sí eolas beacht ar obair Chonradh na Gaeilge' [according to herself this was the time she acquired precise knowledge of the work of *Conradh na Gaeilge*] (Luccan, 1993, 8).

Éilís Ní Thiarnaigh gives the following comprehensive account of what that work was:

> It was a movement that would have no connection to religion or politics ... Hyde and his friends travelled around the country propagating their teachings and trying to encourage the people ... To awaken the people's interest in their aims was some of the most difficult work that had to be done. In the districts where people still had Irish they were reluctant to speak it to people who were educated as they felt that was bad-mannered. In the districts where Irish was only a memory in the minds of the elderly it was difficult to awaken interest in it. Why would anyone bother to learn a language that was only a symbol of poverty and ignorance? (Ní Thiarnaigh, 1970, 32)

Peripatetic teachers travelled the length and breadth of the country propagating the aims of *Conradh na Gaeilge* and teaching Irish through lessons and conversation. *Conradh na Gaeilge* was also a social organization in which men and women could come together in class, at *céilithe* [Irish dances], plays, competitions and *feiseanna* [gatherings]. The men and women in question, from all ages and backgrounds, founded branches throughout the country, enhancing the social life of the districts in question. Although there were only approximately eighty branches in existence in 1899, by 1908 there were in the region of 671 (McMahon, 2008, 88). There were few women on the Executive Committee, however, though it was mostly women who regularly attended the local branch meetings. Many of the women who took part in the Easter Rising 1916 came up through the ranks of *Conradh na Gaeilge*.

As Louise points out, it was during her visit to its office in 1903, that she heard Irish spoken for the first time: proof positive that it existed as a living language and, more than this, that interest in it was growing by the day. It is worth mentioning also that this was the first time a member of *Conradh na Gaeilge* spoke to the young woman who would conceive of the concept of all-Irish education in this country some years afterwards.

However, Louise had to return to France shortly after her visit to Ireland. She had not yet reached the age of majority; she had no means of support; the concept of higher education for women was in its infancy. She also had to heed the stipulations laid down in her father's will.

Gavan Duffy had drawn up his will on 18 November 1898. In it he gave his address as 'Latamard in the County of Mornington in the colony of Victoria', stating that he was 'now for several years, a visitor to Europe but domiciled in Australia' (Gavan Duffy, 1903). Although he had been living in France since 1880, it is clear that he considered these years a sojourn abroad from his permanent home in Australia. Susan and Harriet were named as executors and trustees of his personal estate in Europe and anywhere else outside Australia. His sons, John and Charles Cashel were named executors and trustees of his personal estate and property in Australia.

Susan and Harriet were also named as guardians 'of my infant children till they arrive at the age of twenty one years.' Susan was 56 years of age at the time and Harriet was 44. Gavan Duffy also stipulated that:

> It is my wish that after my death all my daughters and my infant sons shall reside in Australia under the protection of their brothers and that the infant children shall live with the Guardians appointed for them in this will or the survivor of them till the said infants shall have reached the age of twenty one years.

In 1903 George, Louise's older brother, was based in London and articled to a solicitor. Her younger brothers, Bryan and Thomas were attending Stonyhurst, the Jesuit College, which their four older half-brothers had also attended. Louise was the only one of the 'infant children' who would have to move from one hemisphere to the other were she to fulfill her father's wishes. She had met her half-brothers when they visited Nice and had regularly seen photographs of their '*joli bebé, belle jeune fille*, or *gracieuse dame*' (Gavan Duffy, 1894, 33). She had also listened to the stories Susan told her about life in Australia but knew little else about the country. Having travelled Australia in accordance with their father's wishes, Louise and her half-sisters managed to return to Nice by 1905, the year she reached the age of majority. She would have to wait a further two years until, in addition to her father's bequest, an inheritance from her mother's family provided her with economic freedom and enabled her to come to Ireland to study.

> In 1907 I realised my great wish and came to live in Ireland – at first to study at the University. Most girls in those days did not attend lectures in University College; they studied in some of the houses that provided a course and prepared one for University examinations. I went to the Dominican College in Eccles Street and was very happy there. (Gavan Duffy, 1966)

In 1909 the Royal University was dissolved. In its place the previous year Queen's University in Belfast and the National University of Ireland, which comprised colleges in Dublin, Cork and Galway, had been founded. 1908 was the year also in which women were permitted to attend university on an equal footing with men. However, Louise decided to attend the Dominican-run *Coláiste Naomh Muire.*

Louise followed a correspondence course from Cusack's College in London for the Matriculation Examination which she passed in1908; she enrolled in the National University the same year. As well as following the university curriculum, Louise began to take an interest in politics: 'bhí na léachtaí suimiúil, chualathas ráflaí faoi na hÓglaigh agus "Sinn Féin"' [the lectures were interesting and we heard rumours about the Volunteers and Sinn Féin] (Gabhánach Ní Dhufaigh, 1993, 2). She enrolled in *Sinn Féin* and, in 1914, became, along with Mary Colum, one of the first joint secretaries of *Cumann na mBan* [Association of Women].

She joined *An Ardchraobh* [The Head Branch] of *Conradh na Gaeilge* and began to study Irish in University and attend classes in *Conradh na Gaeilge*, both in Dublin and in the Tourmakeady *Gaeltacht*. It was in one of these classes that she caught her first glimpse of Patrick Pearse:

> I had seen Pádraic Pearse once, when he came to examine a Gaelic League class that I was in – and I still remember the vivid impression he made on me – 'A strange arresting man,' I told a friend, 'ugly and so attractive.' (Gavan Duffy, 1966)

Her degree in modern languages was conferred on her by the National University of Ireland in 1911. However, before graduating, she had already been offered a job:

> In the summer I came back from the Gaeltacht, and I was going to have my Degree examination in the autumn of 1911. Mollie Maguire, later Padraig Colum's wife, was teaching in St. Ita's, she had been teaching there since the school opened. She said to me 'we are in difficulties as one of the teachers is leaving. Could you come?' I said, 'I don't know much Irish, and what about this teacher?' Mollie Maguire said, 'She won't come back. She fell out with Mr. Pearse'. (Gavan Duffy, 1949)

Pearse had founded *Scoil Éanna* [Saint Enda's], his school for boys, in Cullenswood House in Ranelagh in 1908. Two years later *Scoil Éanna* moved to a larger premises in Rathfarnham and *Scoil Íde* [Saint Ita's], a school for girls, was established in Cullenswood House. Pearse was headmaster of both schools. The ethos of both schools was patriotic in the extreme: Irish history and myth were taught and the children were indoctrinated with nationalist ideals. Many of the boys would go on to fight in the Easter Rising in 1916.

In 1905 Pearse and his sister, Margaret, had visited Belgium to experience at first hand the bilingual system in which French and Flemish were taught side by side in Belgian schools. He would draw on this model in developing a bilingual Irish and English system in his own schools. Donn Piatt, a pupil and teacher in Scoil Éanna describes this system:

> each language was taught thro' itself, by the Direct Method, in other subjects (except Higher Maths, where there was a lack of textbooks in Irish) a lesson was taught in both languages – first in Irish (or in English), then in English or Irish. (Piatt, 1993, 34–7)

Conradh na Gaeilge had campaigned for a regular system of bilingual instruction in *Gaeltacht* areas to cater for children who had no English before attending their local schools which were all-English in name. Permission for this approach was granted in 1902. The opposite was the case in Dublin where in *Scoil Éanna* most children had no Irish before they attended school.

Louise was delighted to accept the teaching position in *Scoil Íde*: 'tairgeadh post dom i gceann dá chuid scoileanna, Scoil Íde, tar éis dom mo chéim Ollscoile a bhaint amach, ghlac mé leis an tairscint go fonnmhar' [I was offered a position in St Ita's, one of his two schools, after I had been awarded my degree, which I eagerly accepted] (Gabhánach Ní Dhufaigh, 1993, 2).

Though Pearse was headmaster of *Scoil Íde*, the day to day running of the school was left to Gertrude Bloomer and a few other women teachers. Pearse would visit once a fortnight: 'chun ceacht a thabhairt ar stair na hÉireann. B'iontach go deo a bheith ag éisteacht leis na ceachtanna sin agus tá mé cinnte nár chuala aon dream cailíní, roimhe sin ná ó shin ceachtanna staire chomh bríomhar, suimiúil leo siúd' [to give a lesson on the history of Ireland. It was wonderful in the extreme listening to those lessons and I am sure that no group of girls, before or since heard history lessons as lively and interesting] (Gabhánach Ní Dhufaigh, 1993, 2).

The lessons lasted a half an hour

Louise taught in *Scoil Íde* during the academic year 1911–2. However, by May 1912, she had become dissatisfied with the running of the school. She did not approve of the management and felt there were too few teachers. By this time also, both *Scoil Éanna* and *Scoil Íde* were experiencing financial difficulties. Louise sought to remedy the situation. She would buy *Scoil Íde* from Pearse. Though Pearse was delighted with her proposal, both schools were owned by *Scoil Éanna Ltd*, a limited liability company which had been established in January 1912. Louise sought the advice of her brother, George, who had qualified as a solicitor. Correspondence flew backwards and forwards between Louise, George, Pearse and other legal and financial experts representing Pearse during the months May to August 1912, Gavan Duffy, Louise, 'Correspondence relating to a proposal that Louise Gavan Duffy should take over the running of St Ita's' (National Library of Ireland, 1912). It appeared that in addition to buying the school, Louise might be liable for some of its debts. However, much to the relief of her family, Louise failed to buy *Scoil Íde*. Later in the year

Pearse managed to retrieve control of both schools and to keep *Scoil Éanna* open.

Louise returned to college, studied for a teacher's diploma with Cambridge University and began an M.A. on *The Education of Women in the Early Nineteenth Century. Some French Points of View*, Gavan Duffy, Louise, M.A. Thesis (1916), Special Collections, James Joyce Library, UCD. The women whose writings and approaches she studied were Madame Campan, Madame de Rémusat and Madame Guizot, who were involved in education in Restoration France. Her study was interrupted when, while working on her thesis, she heard rumours of the Rising. She went to investigate and spent Easter Week in charge of the kitchen in the GPO.

The following year, 1917, Louise co-founded *Scoil Bhríde* [St Brigid's School], with Eithne McAodha. Scoil Bhríde was the first *Gaelscoil* [all-Irish primary school] in the country. 'She saw the young girls around her with no opportunities for the ideal Irish education which she felt they sought and so with a few pupils she started a private school …' (O'Brennan, 1945, 10). While Pearse had believed in the bilingual approach, she believed in an all-Irish system. She had grown up in Nice, a cosmopolitan city, where most people moved effortlessly between languages. More than that, she had been educated in a school where French was the only language permitted in both classroom and schoolyard.

One of the reasons that Pearse had moved Scoil Éanna to Rathfarnham was that he felt Cullenswood House was: 'so to speak, too much in the Suburban Groove' (Mac Piarais, 1910, 9). Day pupils may well have brought English in on their coat-tails but English was already spoken inside the school walls. In creating an all-Irish school Louise encouraged her students to speak Irish both in the classroom and in the schoolyard, by introducing incentives. Her system of teaching Irish, one of complete immersion in the language, took some years to develop. She explained her modus operandi in an article she wrote for *The Leader* in 1957:

> Our children come to school at the age of four or five – the earlier the better. The great majority of them have no Irish at home … They spend two years in the Infant classes, learning to speak the language by talking, playing, singing – and in general they are blissfully happy and unwilling to miss a day at school … There is no reading or writing taught in the Infant classes of a national school – no lessons in the accepted

> sense of the term; and this fact disposes of most of the talk about 'strain'. These children think of school as a place where you learn to speak Irish. It is all a kind of a game, played by teacher and children, and, on the whole, it is great fun. After two years of it, the average child is quite at home in a simple conversation and is ready for promotion to First Standard, where there will still be no English but where he will begin reading, writing, arithmetic and Christian Doctrine in Irish, the language that he is accustomed to using in school. (Gavan Duffy, 1957, 9–11)

As the twentieth century progressed Irish continued to decline in *Gaeltacht* areas but in the late 1960s began to gather momentum in towns and cities. Although a few schools had hitherto been teaching all subjects through Irish, during these years some parents in urban areas began to demand that their children be educated completely through Irish. The number of *gaelscoileanna* increased rapidly; these were followed by *naíonraí* [pre-schools], and second-level schools, meaning that children in urban areas could be schooled exclusively through Irish between the ages of 3 and 18.

The fact that she herself had been denied secondary education was an obvious factor in Louise's choice of subject matter for her MA thesis which focused on the work of women pioneers in the education of girls in France, the country where she was born and where she grew up. The subject matter was portentous also: it encompassed the study of both the written and practical work of women who lived during France's *ancien régime*, who survived the Revolution and found favour with the subsequent administration during the Restoration years. Louise survived a revolution in her own country and went on to found a new educational enterprise and develop a new educational system within the Irish Free State. Her love of Irish, her native language which had been denied her as a child, was another driving force as she set about establishing her new all-Irish teaching system.

The work which Louise's father did on *The Nation* had the effect of spreading the use of English during the mid-nineteenth century. In 1917, seventy years later, his daughter co-founded a school in which every subject was taught through Irish. She created a movement which provided an educational framework through which new generations of urban speakers of Irish could emerge. The number of *gaelscoileanna* in the country continues to grow. Today, on the island of Ireland, there are 254 naíonraí, 305 primary and seventy-one secondary all-Irish schools.

It was Louise Gavan Duffy who conceived of the idea of teaching all subjects through Irish. While it might not be true to say that, without her, this might not have happened, it is true to say that it did happen and that it was she who caused it to happen.

Bibliography

Conway, Gerry (2017). 'Irish-medium early years state of the sector report', <https://www.altram.org/sites/default/files/AltramExecutiveSummary_FINAL_Su%C3%ADomh.pdf>, accessed 26 August 2018.

De h-Íde, Dubhghlas (1937). *Mise agus an Connradh* (Baile Átha Cliath: Oifig Dhíolta Foilseacháin Rialtais).

Gabhánach Ní Dhufaigh, Lúise (1993). 'Ag insint a scéil féin', in Mairéad Ní Ghacháin, ed., *Lúise Gabhánach Ní Dhufaigh agus Scoil Bhríde* (Baile Átha Cliath: Coiscéim), 1–7.

Gaelscoileanna Teoranta (n.d.). 'Provision of Irish-medium Education, September 2017', <http://www.gaelscoileanna.ie/en/about/statistics/>, accessed 26 August 2018.

Gavan Duffy, Charles (1898). *My Life in Two Hemispheres* (London: T. Fisher Unwin).

—— (1903). 'Last Will and Testament' (Monaghan: County Museum, Monaghan).

Gavan Duffy, Louise (1912). Papers. 'Correspondence relating to a proposal that Louise Gavan Duffy should take over the running of St Ita's' (MS 46, 553/1–2: National Library of Ireland).

—— (1916). 'The Education of Women in the early Nineteenth Century. Some French Points of View' (MA Thesis, Special Collections, James Joyce Library, UCD).

—— (1949). 'Witness Statement 216' (Bureau of Military History, Department of Defence).

—— (1957). 'Teaching Through Irish', *The Leader* 57/23, 9–11.

—— (1966). Papers, 'Self Portrait' (MS 46,271: National Library of Ireland).

Gavan Duffy, Susan (1894). *The English Abroad: Sketched by an Australian Cousin (S.G. Duffy)* (London: T. Fisher Unwin).

Luccan, Nóra (1993). 'An Bhean Tréitheach', in Mairéad Ní Ghacháin, ed., *Lúise Gabhánach Ní Dhufaigh agus Scoil Bhríde* (Baile Átha Cliath: Coiscéim), 8–10.

Mac Piarais, Pádraic (1910). 'By Way of Comment', *An Macaomh*, 2/3, 9–19.
MacDonagh, Oliver (1983). *States of Mind: A Study of Anglo-Irish Conflict, 1780–1980* (London: Allen and Unwin).
McMahon, Timothy G. (2008). *Grand Opportunity: The Gaelic Revival and Irish Society, 1893–1910* (Syracuse, NY: Syracuse University Press).
Ní Ghacháin, Mairéad, ed. (1993). *Lúise Gabhánach Ní Dhufaigh agus Scoil Bhríde* (Baile Átha Cliath: Coiscéim).
Ní Thiarnaigh, Éilís (1970). *Casadh na Taoide, 1891–1925* (Baile Átha Cliath: Foilseacháin Náisiúnta Teoranta).
Ó Broin, Leon (1967). *Charles Gavan Duffy: Patriot and Statesman* (Dublin: James Duffy & Co,).
Ó Glaisne, Risteárd (1991). *Dúbhghlas de h-Íde (1860–1849): Ceannródaí Cultúrtha* (Baile Átha Cliath: Conradh na Gaeilge).
O'Brennan, Kathleen (1945). 'Louise Gavan Duffy', *The Leader* 90/25, 10–11.
Piatt, Donn (1993). 'Gearrchuntas ar Stair Scoil Bhríde', in Mairéad Ní Ghacháin, ed., *Lúise Gabhánach Ní Dhufaigh agus Scoil Bhríde* (Baile Átha Cliath: Coiscéim), 34–7.

BRENDA MURPHY

4 Media landscapes and striptease cultures: Patriarchy, portrayal and bodies

> Much has changed for women since I was a little girl in the 1950s in New York City. In many places the lives and spaces of women and men have become less separate, and women fill roles and appear in places that might have surprised my grandmother. For all that, the image of woman has not ceased being that of the Other: the surface that reflects fantasies and fears arising from our human being as vulnerable bodies. Just because images and expectations about women make us asymmetrically associated with sex, birth, age, and flesh, we have little voice to express our own point of view on this fleeting existence or on the social relations that position us. (Young 2005: 3)

Iris Young begins her essay *On Female Body Experience, Throwing Like a Girl* with this positive statement that alludes to the shifts that have taken place socially and culturally around women's lived experiences. The lives and spaces of women and men have become less separate, and women, to varying degrees, fill roles and appear in places that they were previously absent from.

Occupying spaces

Women increasingly occupy decision making positions in public life, in corporate and finance, and in legislative roles. However, their words, actions, achievements and contributions are rarely featured in the news, and these successful role models are seldom reflected in other genres in the media such as movies, sit coms or advertising. Indeed, if we scrutinize the media (media production, media portrayal and the media industry) *where women fill roles and appear* (Young, Opening Quote (ibid.)) these remain hugely contested spaces where women are absent, under represented, or portrayed in narrow stereotypical poses and characterizations.

Drawing on data collected as part of the 2015 Global Media Monitoring Project (GMMP) Ross et al. (2016) argue that since the first GMMP (1995) the proportion of women who report, present, or are subjects in the news has risen slowly over those twenty years by 7 per cent to a heady 24 per cent. Visibility is only a part of the problem, and Ross et al. observe that when women are present, their contributions are often confined to the private as they are reported in the role of citizen rather than expert and women are mostly reported in stories about health but not politics. They noted just over a third of the media professionals coded were women and older women are significant in their absence.

So while in many places *the lives and spaces of women and men have become less separate* (Young, Opening Quote (ibid.)) and women are increasingly occupying positions, spaces and places, when we look to the mediatized spaces on screen, in digital broadcast and print, the hazy inaccurate reflections of 'the real world' which the media is supposedly mirroring is *not* reflecting women as occupying decision making positions or holding power. In the many places women occupy and reside *the image of woman has not ceased being that of the Other: the surface that reflects fantasies and fears arising from our human being as vulnerable bodies* (Young, Opening Quote (ibid.)).

Ideologies, dominant ideologies and patriarchy

In this chapter I argue that the seditious and devious process of devaluation and disempowerment of women takes place subtly, through patriarchal discursive practices. These can be found in media conduct everywhere we look. But to understand how patriarchal practices work, it is useful to look first at the mechanisms behind ideologies and how they function.

Thompson (2016) defines ideologies as those fixed sets of ideas that are linked with a particular set of social arrangements and by attaching to norms and values within society, they have the effect of legitimating the status quo – justifying protecting and reinforcing those social arrangements and the subsequent inherent power relations. For example, patriarchal ideology promotes the notion of traditional roles for men and women and discourages any deviations. Power interests inherent in patriarchy are therefore well served by the ideology of patriarchy. For Thompson, the ideas base safeguards the power base.

Patriarchy is one of the most successful ideologies as its influence and reward is global. Other ideologies are limited by political and geographic landscapes but, I argue, patriarchy operates around a binary logic of them: us, empowered: disempowered, and men: women. It occupies and defines almost every sphere of life and it prevails as a system of society, culture and government in which men define and hold power and women are largely excluded from it. Indeed the reproduction of patriarchy is sustained and can be quickly located in and around unequal workloads and unequal rewards. It continues to be characterized by unequal power relations between women and men where women are systematically disadvantaged; And where women in minority groups face further and multiple oppressions (currently and historically) as race, class and sexuality intersect. For the purpose of this chapter I coin and use the term *Project Patriarchy* as a shortcut-reference to the all-encompassing, mostly unexamined practices that coalesce around patriarchy.

Recipe for a successful dominant ideology

Ideologies are upheld by numerous mechanisms or pillars and in this story, we are focusing on patriarchal ideologies. Althusser (1971) in his essay 'Ideology and Ideological State Apparatuses', differentiates between two mechanisms which sustain ideologies: the repressive state apparatus (RSA), that is, the police, army and legal structures, and ideological state apparatuses (ISA), that is, private institutions such as schools (education), the church (religion), the family, political systems (including different parties), cultural (literature, the arts, sports, etc.) and the mass media. These organizations disseminate beliefs that are less obviously 'coming from above', are more heterogeneous in shape, and occupy private realms of existence. While the RSAs function primarily by oppression or violence, and secondarily by ideology, the Ideological State Apparatuses function by ideology and secondarily by punishment or control. Althusser explains that in ISAs (school, church, family and culture) expulsion, selection, exclusion and censorship function to discipline transgressors or opponents and reward devotees.

For Althusser, the educational apparatus replaced the church as its primary dominant ideological state apparatus and argues that each group of individuals leaves the system at key moments – manual labourers leave the system early, the *petit bourgeoisie* leave after their first degree and leaders complete further specialist training – and they all join the work force with the ideology necessary for the reproduction of the current system. Each group is takes with them the correct ideology to perform that role in society. However in contemporary society education is not the only scriptwriter writing on each group. The church, the family, culture and the media coalesce to uphold the values of the dominant ideology internally, and they reinforce the script for all so it is very difficult to escape or extract yourself from it. Sometimes utterly unaware, they work together they uphold the patriarchal project.

Mediatized ideologies

Drawing together the threads of ideologies, dominant ideologies, and patriarchy – I hold that the media is a cornerstone in the success of *Project Patriarchy*, the oldest surviving project in town. Mediatization – the relationship between the media and society – was coined by Hjarvard (2013) and described a social process where society is saturated and inundated by the media to the extent that the media cannot be thought of separate from other institutions within the society. Hjarvard argues that while the media does not necessarily 'cause' the transformations they are co-conspirators – aiding the articulation of politics, economics, education, religion, etc. Hjarvard gave the example of television programmes where health specialists promote quick individual changes in lifestyle and thus co-construct the notion of health together with other institutions and broader cultural shifts around perceptions of the body.[1]

I maintain that society is so saturated and inundated by the media, more so with the rapidly multiplying power of digital media and social media – that it has become successfully woven into the daily fabric of our existence, bring with it, other social institutions – all of them hallmarked with patriarchal ideologies.

Mechanisms that uphold *Project Patriarchy*

Project Patriarchy is identifiable by many markers but one of the most profound is the use and power of the gaze, of looking, being looked at, being positioned to look in a certain way. While this chapter explores how the media functions to uphold patriarchy as a dominant ideology, I argue that one particular dimension of the dynamic of power is propped up and sustained around a very particular process which can be located in the way women are portrayed, represented and appear and how they are positioned and framed in the media, in the process of production; and how those images are read or decoded or deconstructed, in the process of

1 In a useful summary Hjarvard and Peterson describe the media's role in cultural change: '(a) when subcultures harness media for their own purposes, they can become (re-)embedded into mainstream culture; (b) national policies often serve as levers for increased mediatization; (c) mediatization involves a transformation of the ways in which authority and expertise are performed and reputation is acquired and defended; and (d) technological progress shapes media affordance (i.e. the way it is seen or experienced) and subsequently, a particular path of mediatization.'

reading and meaning making. The representation and subsequent myths are projected into the world for all of us to absorb.

The term 'gaze' is complex and may not fully capture the essence of the process. Mulvey invokes the male gaze; American scholars talk about lookism; Berger refers to looked at ness but none of these terms fully embrace the process that positions women in the mediatized world. The term and construct 'gaze' has crossed disciplines and time.

Gazing at histories

In critical theory, sociology and psychoanalysis the concept of the gaze describes the act of seeing and being seen. In 1963 Foucault developed the concept of the gaze to illustrate how power relations work in medical scenarios between doctors and patients, where a power dynamic prevails, and in 1975, as an apparatus of power around surveillance and self-regulation in prisons and schools.

In 1975 Mulvey wrote of the male gaze which was embraced as a feminist media term, and in 1990 Butler proposed the feminine gaze.[2] In 1996 Kaplan introduced the concept of the imperial gaze (which is inextricably linked with the postcolonial gaze) in which the observed find themselves defined in terms of the privileged observer's own set of values. Her work addressed race and power relations and argued that 'looking relations' are determined by history, tradition and myth; and by national identity, power hierarchies, politics, economics and geography. Kaplan's work was a response to critics around white feminist film theory in the 1970s and 1980s where race was neglected. Kaplan retains the construct of 'the male gaze' but applies it across cultures. In 1992 bell hooks introduced the oppositional gaze of Black women – to counter Mulvey's notion of the male gaze.

2 In Gender Trouble 1990 Butler proposed the idea of the feminine gaze as a way in which men choose to perform their masculinity by using women as the ones who force men into self-regulation.

Said (1991) refers to orientalism, colonial discourse and to a postcolonial gaze, where the colonized is in a position of 'other'. The gaze functions by establishing a subject/object relationship and the colonizer:colonized relationship is defined by the colonizer's role and power relations. Urry (1992) talked of the 'romantic, and the collective tourist gaze, but revisits the concept and expands it to include spectatorial, environmental and anthropological and in 2000 Prichard and Morgan engage a feminist analysis of tourism where they critique the role of gender relations in the production and consumption of tourism experiences and images. They develops the concept of gendered tourism landscapes and discusses the interrelationship between the language of patriarchy and (hetero) sexuality and the language of tourism promotion, and they concluded that the language and imagery of promotion privileges the male, heterosexual gaze. In 2012 Winch talks about how, in the 'hyper-visible landscape of popular culture, the feminine ideal is the girl and the girled body is an asset'. She introduces the concept of the girlfriend gaze, and she argues that 'girlfriendship places women's friendship at the core of feminine identities. The male gaze is rendered benign with men cast as an accessory to improve a girl's worth to the most important people in her life, her friends. Girlfriendships are exploited for the mutual governance of this feminine ideal as women prove their worth for the approbation of other women. Through doing so, they are complicit in perpetuating discourses of misogyny' (2010: 21).

Sturken and Cartwright in *Practices of Looking* (2009) argue that the gaze is conceptually central to systems of power and to ideas about knowledge. They argue that the act of gazing produces personal relationship with the person being looked at. Foucault developed the concept of panopticism, where institutional surveillance promotes self-surveillance and regulation of the self. The media, as an institution which functions to uphold a wide range of ideologies, has embedded within it a whole range of, and processes of, looking, gazing and surveillance.

Lutz and Collins (1991) review Mulvey and Berger's standpoint and note that they alert us to how the position of the spectator has the potential to enhance or articulate the power of the observer over the observed. And they offer several critiques – such as the unique vision of the female spectator whose view is seen as multiple because, it can move between identification with the object and the spectator, and may be equated to an oppositional gaze, since, and they cite Williams (1991: 135), it 'disrupts the authority and closure of dominant representations.' They identify a multitude of gazes – the photographer's gaze, the magazine's gaze, the magazine reader's gaze, a western gaze, the non-western subject's gaze, the refracted gaze of the other, to see themselves as others see them.

Mediatized gaze, mediatized bodies, embodiment and subjectification

The media works well and hard, every day, to produce particular versions of the world and particular versions of gendered bodies. The persistently recurring moments of portrayal produce and reproduce a particular ideology, which is difficult to escape. The scripts for our embodiment are upheld by numerous mechanisms or pillars that support dominant (in this case patriarchal) ideologies. For Althusser, the media is one of those pillars and I argue that through patriarchal discursive practices there is a systematic process of devaluation and disempowerment that women are subject to. As discussed above the media is a powerful mechanism that supports patriarchal myths and one of those powerful myths is 'lookism/gaze/surveillance'.

Appearance is a 'gendered' issue

Our bodies constantly 'appear', and how we 'appear' matters. Our experiences of 'appearing' and 'being' in our bodies is a gendered experience. The process of appearing and 'being looked at' are complex and deeply rooted in our gendered world. Women and men occupy, are portrayed and appear in the world and in the media-world in different ways ... and are subjected to different expressions of portrayal. A perfect example of this is manner in which female politicians are portrayed by the media. The stereotypical framings of women in public life are: invisible women; health and education are suitable issues for women; always married with children; style over substance; gendered speech: men say, women blast; negative gender distinctions, frames and metaphors (*Portraying Politics* 2006).

For example in March 2017 the *Daily Mail* featured Theresa May, Prime Minister in the UK, and Nicola Sturgeon, First Minister in Scotland, on the front page of the paper with the headline 'Never mind Brexit, who won Legs-it!' and fills the front page with a picture of May and Sturgeon, sitting in armchairs. The shot was taken from a mid- to low point in order to emphasize their legs (Figure 4.1).

Daily Mail

TUESDAY, MARCH 28, 2017

NEWSPAPER OF THE YEAR 65p

Never mind Brexit, who won Legs-it!

It wasn't quite stilettos at dawn, but there was a distinctly frosty atmosphere when Theresa May met Nicola Sturgeon yesterday

SEE PAGES 6-7

Figure 4.1: *The Daily Mail*, 28 March 2017

But women, no matter what role they play in society, in political life or elsewhere, are systematically exposed to 'valuation' around how they appear.

Moments of resistance: Avoiding the gaze

We have all experienced of the gaze and its power – as encoders or decoders, surveyors or surveyed. As women intersect around race, class, ethnicity and gender, they express their responses in many ways – discomfort, anger, irritation and annoyance, and thanks to the power of social scripting, with pleasure of being looked at, admired and valued for social qualities around appearance.

Australian singer Sia has done her bit for political activism at various points in her career and for many years she concealed her face during performances and interviews to avoid a celebrity lifestyle and maintain some privacy. It may seem paradoxical for an artist, who is dependent on being observed and reported on to ensure success, to decide to hide her face. In an interview in 2015 she said 'I'm trying to have some control over my image. And I'm allowed to maintain some modicum of privacy. But also I would like not to be picked apart or for people to observe when I put on ten pounds or take off ten pounds or I have a hair extension out of place or my fake tan is botched. Most people don't have to be under that pressure, and I'd like to be one of them' (*Interview Magazine* 2015; Figure 4.2).

When an artist who is residing in and dependent on the rules of popular culture chooses to hide her face and her identity we are prompted to look closer at the statement she is making. Historically and contemporarily when women 'appear' they are signified as bodies and go on to become regulated bodies, modified bodies and policed bodies. They are constructed around appearance and location – as public bodies: private bodies; bodies as performance, bodies as commodity, boundaried bodies (allowed to be here, not there) and constructed as female bodies, male

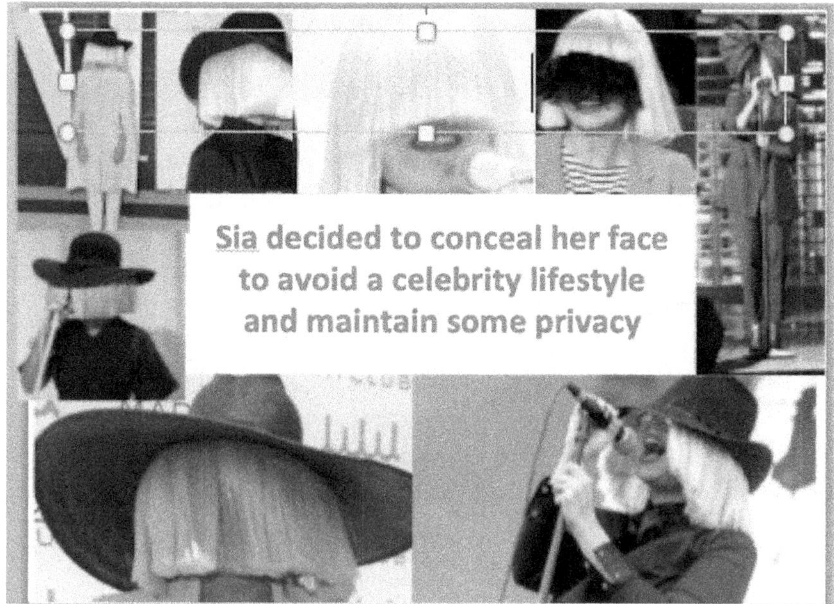

Figure 4.2: Sia performing in various places – montage of images [online]

bodies, ethnic bodies, othered bodies, able:disabled bodies, etc. And in academia, there are many sites where the body is theorized – psychology of the body, sociology of the body, politicialization of the body, and history of the body (Turner 1996).

Spaces, power and control

The body is transformed into a site as the process and act of surveillance occur, and it becomes a contested and complex space where power and control enter the story and expressions of power are employed around 'the body'. These expressions of control and power are located in physical and imagined places, exerting mental boundaries and physical boundaries.

Examples of physical spaces are numerous and they are bound by social, cultural, religious and legislative mores. Cultural and social mores impact just as powerfully as religious, state and legislative edicts. Unwritten rules prevail; for example, generationally a 60-year-old woman is less likely to feel comfortable entering a pub alone as she perceives it as a male space (Murphy 2015), and the last of the 'men-only pubs' is still a living memory for many. Women and men sat in different sections of the (Catholic) church in Ireland, and continued to do so in rural areas up to 1970s and in 2019 mosques continue to retain one space for men and another for women.

Discursive practices in the media

The media is located in a cultural and social space of its own making and its own definition, where bodies coalesce and the notions of control become even more complex and subtle. How bodies are portrayed and appear, are part of a particular set of discursive practices – practices that are ideologically driven and patriarchal in origin.

The prevailing media images of women (and lately, but to a lesser extent, men) on screen and in print, it is easy to locate the (albeit essentialist understanding of sexualization) 'striptease culture' coined by McNair (2002) that has grown and become mainstream. Images of females (and sometimes males) have become hypersexualized (Connell, 2005; Kimmel, Hearn and Connell, 2005), commodified (Bordo, 1993), produced and reproduced (cosmetically and technically) into spectacles of unattainable 'beauty ideals' (Wolf, 1990) and 'perfect bodies'.

While the media industry produces particular versions of the world, it also produces particular versions of bodies and it uses those framings to produce an endless sweeping landscape or world of messages and myths around gendered power relations. These images, signs and myths, and the meaning making that is both generating and receiving them is fuelled by and for *Project Patriarchy*.

Alongside the encounter with the images, the parasitic and automatic act of 'looking' must occur and when the gaze takes place the encoding begins. Audiences/ readers/ consumers/ citizens – whatever collective that is most useful to consider and personally comfortable to identify with – women and men alike – all meet and greet the images and messages through an act of looking. That act of looking, that gaze, now dripping with the complex processes of comprehension (what the image means to me and what I've been socialized to understand by that image), positioning (where that image places me in relation to the subject of the gaze) and active belief (this is the status quo that we uphold) or resistance (I hate the way s/he is being portrayed) is the final stage of meaning making. The portrayals encompass and reproduce a particular ideology which is very difficult to escape from.

Gendered Stereotypes

Within the act of looking or gazing and meaning making, the reader is often met with stereotypical shortcuts that safeguard accurate decoding and ensure preferred readings (Hall 1980), that is, reading or decoding in keeping with the prevailing or dominant ideology. No matter what domain, format or genre, women and men are anchored to a (sometimes changing) set of meanings that are in themselves anchored by the use of stereotyping. The mechanism can be found wherever there is media coverage – women as politicians, as athletes, in the cast of movies (comedy, drama, horror, Noir, etc.), in the news (GMMP), in roles depicting occupations, children's programmes and cartoons. Some of those stereotypes are:

- objectification – reducing women to 'an object' where their body or parts of their body 'stand for something else' – a bottle of vodka, a piece of jewelry or some other commodity.
- the cult of thinness – where thin is paramount, and the ideal body is thin. Only 8 per cent of women look like EVERY FEMALE in advertising – and

Kilbourne argues that the 'ideal' body doesn't actually exist – it is a product of surgery, cosmetics and digital editing (Adobe Photoshop, etc.).

- the beauty myth – which Wolf (1990) defines as an obsession with physical perfection that traps the women in an endless spiral of hope, self-consciousness, and self-hatred in order to live up to the impossible social definition of 'beauty'. She argues that the beauty myth is the last and best belief system that works to keep male dominance in place.
- women as consumers: men as producers (of media content, and of commodities).
- women and violence – the prevailing stereotype in news and other programming is of women as victim – usually as a result of gender-based violence – women seldom kill or hurt other women, women are more likely to be hurt or killed by men.
- active boys and men: passive girls and women – this binary stereotype is found in many media spaces – in toy adverts, cartoons, drama productions, etc., and roles played by men: women. The way those roles are framed and edited further expresses the stereotype – fast moving, upbeat music, short clips and outdoor action reinforce the 'active boy' stereotype, while longer cuts and soft, slow music, indoor activities mark the passive girl stereotype. Indeed research on print media for children such as storybooks reveals the prevalent gender stereotypes where males were more active; gender stereotypes were common; gender neutral behaviours were more likely to be done by males. Females were more likely to be depicted as children and humans; whereas males were mostly depicted as animals, adults, and superheroes (Fitzpatrick and McPherson, 2010).
- absent or silent and nonspeaking adds up to invisibility or symbolic annihilation[3] (Gerbner, 1976; Tuchman, 1978).
- hypersexualized women are often sexualized – typically by showing them in scanty or provocative clothing (Collins, 2011).

3 The term symbolic annihilation was first used by George Gerbner in order to describe the absence of representation, or underrepresentation, of some group of people in the media (often based on their race, sex, sexual orientation, socio-economic status, etc.), as a means of maintaining inequality and was applied to media criticism. Gaye Tuchman (1978) divided the concept into three aspects: omission, trivialization and condemnation and this approach to coverage vilifies communities of identity and works to make members invisible through the explicit lack of representation in all forms of media ranging from film, song, books, news media and visual art.

- subordinated women are also subordinated in various ways, as indicated by their facial expressions, body positions, and other factors. Finally, they are shown in traditionally feminine (i.e. stereotyped) roles (Collins, 2011).
- occupationally/role devalued – women are portrayed as non-professionals, homemakers, wives or parents, and sexual gatekeepers (Collins, 2011).
- ageism – older women are conspicuous in their absence or narrow range of often unflattering stereotypes such as an interfering mother or mother-in-law, or a 'gossip' (Gill, 2007).
- women outside the heterosexual norm are not seen except problematically in highly sexualized portrayal (Gill, 2007).
- black women are frequently portrayed in crude stereotypes signaling animalistic sexuality, exotic 'otherness' or 'soul' – with women of African origin use to play on themes of 'darkness and sexuality' – Tia Maria and Options, and women of Asian origin framed in roles where sexual submissiveness and sexual services are often indexed – see airline adverts, for example (Gill, 2007).

The stereotypes are numerous and they are limiting for women and men.

Interrogating the evidence: Advertising

Kilbourne (1999; 2000; 2002) identifies specific issues as problematic portrayal in advertising, and she has focused on the following issues:

- Objectification;
- Dismemberment;
- The thin 'ideal' perfect body;
- Ageism;
- Infantilization of women;
- Sexualization of young girls;
- Symbolic silencing;
- Trivialization of power;
- Binaries of race and power;
- 'Pornografication' of everyday images;
- Violence against women.

These stereotypes can be found 'all over the media', across formats and genres and there are volumes of studies that identify these media sins. Sexist and problematic media is often cited in advertising and it is arguably one of the most researched media spaces and media texts.

Interrogating the evidence is important and is best done by employing textual analysis which offers powerful methodological tools which can be applied to unsettle a prevailing status quo such as semiotics, content analysis, discourse analysis, etc. This chapter is informed and driven by semiotics in order to interrogate first, second and third readings of media texts in order to identify patriarchal discursive practices and locate ideological constructs that perpetuate gendered bodies and the politics of appearance.

Semiotics and ideology

French philosopher and key thinker in social semiotics, Roland Barthes distinguished between different orders of signification and differentiated between denotation and connotation. He explained them in terms of levels of representation or levels of meaning.

The first order of signification (*denotation*) is, for example, the photograph of the car which means the car, and meaning is framed in terms of what the photo denotes. Writing specifically about photography, Barthes, in the 'Rhetoric of the Image' (1977) argues that in photography the denoted (first-order) meaning is conveyed through the mechanical process of reproduction.

In the next space for meaning production, the second order signification (*connotation*) is generated from experiences we have had and associations (connotations) we have learnt and bring to the sign. There is a whole range of possibilities within those connotations and they are dependent on and a product of the culture and sign-systems we live in and operate. In photography, Barthes argues that connotative (second-order) meanings are introduced by human intervention – lighting, pose, camera angle, etc.

Barthes argues that the orders of signification called denotation and connotation combine to produce ideology – and this has been described (though not by Barthes) as a third order of signification (Chandler 2007).

Third-order signification is a matter of the cultural meanings of signs. These cultural meanings derive not from the sign itself, but from the way that society uses and values the signifier and the signified. To make meaning we draw meanings from the stock of images, notions, concepts and myths which are already available in a particular cultural context and at a particular time. In Barthes's view the myth functions to legitimize dominant ideology and present to us a 'reality' which retains that status quo so that the values incorporated in that 'reality' appear to be quite natural, taken for granted, unquestioned or challenged.

For Barthes, myths serve the ideological function of naturalization (Barthes 1977: 45–6). They work to naturalize the culture, to make dominant cultural and historical values, attitudes and beliefs seem entirely 'natural', 'normal', self-evident, timeless, obvious 'common-sense' – and thus objective and 'true' reflections of 'the way things are'. Sociologists argue that social groups tend to regard as natural whatever confers privilege and power upon themselves. Barthes saw myth as serving the ideological interests of the bourgeoisie and 'bourgeois ideology ... turns culture into nature' (Barthes 1974: 206).

Barthes gave priority to connotation, and in 1971 noted that it was no longer easy to separate the signifier from the signified or the literal from the ideological (Barthes 1977), and while Fiske warns that it is dangerously possible to read connotative meanings as denotative facts or truths (Fiske 1982) it also dangerously possible to accept denotation as the 'literal', 'self-evident' 'truth' (Chandler 2007). Semiotic analysis can help us to counter routinized thinking and unsettle the status quo.

Advertising content systematically draws on the stereotypes detailed by Kilbourne (above) and none of them would function as they do without the aid of the gaze and its rules of engagement. However in 2017/18 the gaze was played out in an even more convoluted way. Advertising agency Energy BBDO/CLM BBDO produced Pants for the Wrigley/Orbit Extra Time to Shine Campaign and the advert that took the gaze to another place.

Decoding the gaze

According to Chandler (2007) it is important to identify the text and describe the medium used and the genre to which the text belongs – this text was a screen based advert, broadcast, in this context, on Irish TV, and it was an advert for Wrigley/Orbit Gum. It was part of a series of four adverts – 'Time to Shine' – where the gum is extracted in socially difficult/ridiculous situations, as the solution to the problem.

I decode the text and explore the discourses at work within the advert by examining the connotations and looking at the activation of meanings deeply rooted in our culture. Taking on the role of 'specialist reader' (Johnson 1983), I deconstruct the advert using semiotics, which enabled me to explore meanings and readings embedded in the text. In *Decoding Advertising*, Judith Williamson (1988) made the liberating argument that we 'are an army of semioticians', able to decode and make meaning. Not everyone will have access to the 'jargon' of semiotics, but the observations made are as relevant as any 'expert readers' observations. In keeping with Williamson's position I extend the act of reading and decoding and invite a small 'sample' of online readers to share their meaning making too. Their deconstructions appear later in this section, following my own analysis.

> The Ad: Wrigley/Orbit Extra Time to Shine. Pants – 20 sec. TV Ad (Ireland) [<https://www.youtube.com/watch?v=abVP6UuBAhM>]
>
> 'The television advertisement depicts a couple, Lucy and Tom, kissing on a bed. A man calls "Lucy" from outside the room and the Lucy says "that's my dad". The couple jump off the bed and Lucy throws Tom's jeans to him. Tom removes chewing gum from the pocket of the jeans and places a piece in his mouth. The door opens to reveal Lucy's parents. Tom standing in his underwear states "Hi I'm Tom" and the father starts to smile.'

Following complaints from audiences, this is how the Australian Advertising Standards (2018) described the advert in its Case Report. They provided what Barthes would call a denotative description, detailing the scene and the script.

However a semiotic analysis looks a little different, it contains more detail and comments on nuances other than a simple 'description' of the advert and its content. It goes beyond a denotative or 'first reading' as seen above, and delves into the meanings or connotations which are located in second and third readings.

Scene 1

Denotative reading: The advert begins in the first the scene. It opens with a young couple in a bedroom, lying on the bed, kissing. It is a 'head and upper body shot'. He is positioned above her and is not wearing a shirt. She is lying on her back on the bed, positioned beneath the boy. She is wearing a shirt.

Connotative readings: In the version of advert that was aired on mainstream TV in Ireland its opening frame contains the young couple lying on a bed, kissing (<https://www.youtube.com/watch?v=abVP6UuBAhM>*). It is not possible to put an accurate age on the couple but the first reading suggests that they are teens and they are in the girl's bedroom, in the girls' family home. The youthfulness of the girl is underlined by the teddy/soft toy on the pillow. The positioning of the bodies is sexual missionary pose with the girl lying back completely on her back, the boy over her and facing down. In other versions of the advert there is additional contextual information. For example the older couple are seen arriving at the University and there is a banner at the University, which reads 'Parent's Day'. This marks that couple as 'parents'. It also situates the younger couple as university students not teens. However in the absence of these contextualizing markers, the meaning generated from the opening scene is very different. These may have been later edits, following complaints, or they may have been cuts to afford a 20 sec ad. Whatever the reason, it demonstrates beautifully and is a perfect example of the power of 'pre-reading cue's which can anchor or change meaning in a text.*

Scene 2

Denotative reading: We hear a knock on the bedroom door, and a man's voice calls 'Hey Lucy'. The camera zooms in on the bedroom door.

Connotative readings: We now have a name for the young female – she is Lucy. She is named by the voice that turns out to be her father. The boyfriend, in later scenes, names himself.

Scene 3
Denotative reading: Lucy looks to the door, mouth open. 'It's my Dad'. Her hand is on his chest in a 'stop' gesture.

Connotative readings: Lucy, on hearing the knock and her dad calling, looks to the door and then back to her boyfriend. They look at each other. The music gets louder and the percussion beats faster. These sounds act as signifiers for 'panic' and 'hurry'.

Scene 4
Denotative reading: In the next scene, the boyfriend is framed alone, standing with his hand out saying 'my jeans'. Camera cuts to Lucy who throws the jeans across the room to him.

Connotative readings: In this scene, the boyfriend is standing in the centre of the room, in control and giving command. An imperative comment – 'my jeans' – is communicated as pass me my jeans quickly. Lucy does so.

Scene 5
Denotative reading: He reaches into his pocket and takes out his gum. As he reaches into the pocket, and that shot takes up most of the screen, Lucy is in the background pulling on her jeans.

Connotative readings: At this point the boyfriend seems to have a plan. He takes the gum out of the front pocket of his jeans. Our gaze and focus is on him and we barely see Lucy in the background.

Scene 6
Denotative reading: There is a still shot of the product. The packet is held between the boy's thumb and forefinger, ensuring a clear 'read' of the packet. Lucy is still framed in the background now fastening her jeans.

Connotative readings: The pause – to view the product – is incongruous. It interrupts the story but its function is to reinforce the role of the product. Placements normally take place at the beginning and/or end of an advert. To interrupt the 'drama' with the product, suggests that it is the solution to the problem/situation. This is what the advertiser wants us to connect with – the gum = 'a time to shine'.

Scene 7

Denotative reading: The boyfriend looks/gazes at the piece of gum into his mouth. He is framed in the foreground, Lucy is to the right of the screen, looking at him, as he looks to camera.

Connotative readings: All the vectors draw us to the boyfriend, who has just put a piece of gum in his mouth. We are compelled to look at him because of the location of his body in the frame, and further compelled as the only other eyes in the shot, Lucy's, look to him too. The message in the narrative is that this is all about the boyfriend. He is central to the story, the plot, and the solution and outcome.

Scene 8

Denotative reading: In the next shot, Tom opens the door and we see his shoulder and part of the back of his head. As the door opens we first see Lucy's Dad staring at the boyfriend, and as the door opens fully, a woman whom we assume to be Lucy's mother. She also stares at the boy. We view Lucy's father as he looks first at the boys' face and then his gaze drops lower. Then the camera switches place and taking the father's gaze, pans up to view the rest of the scene.

Connotative readings: This scene is saturated with multiple gazes with multiple meanings. We as viewers, watch the scene 'over the boyfriend's shoulder'. We see Lucy's parents as they stare at the boyfriend. They look serious and are unsmiling. And they are wide eyed which serves as a signifier for 'surprise'. The viewers/consumers/audience is placed in a subjective position. Although we are looking AT the father, we are compelled to view the scene from his gaze as we watch his eyes move. As readers we have to fill in gaps in order to make meaning and we are drawn to conclude that he is now looking at his pants.

Scene 9

Denotative reading: The camera now frames the boyfriend in the foreground – in a dismembered shot – showing just lower abdomen, boxer shorts and upper legs. We see Lucy in the background but again a shot where she is dismembered – showing just her jeans and bare feet.

The camera then pans upwards, now framing the boyfriend's upper body and face. He gazes back at the callers. Lucy is still in the background, one arm in front of her torso, the other holding the back of her neck. The boy smiles and greets the callers. 'Hi, I'm Tom' he says.

Connotative readings: Now we take the father's view. We are standing beside him at the door viewing the scene. To reinforce the previous scene, we now actually see what was intimated in the previous scene. We look at the boyfriend, at his lower body, and then at his face, as he looks back. His expression can be interpreted in many ways – confident, cocky, sneering, open, friendly – Lucy, in the background holds a non-expressive expression. The boyfriend looks 'at' the father, then in a slight drop of his gaze, to indicate a height difference, he looks 'at' the mother. He says 'Hi, I'm Tom'.

Scene 10

Denotative reading: We now see a head and shoulders shot of Lucy's father. He takes up 2/3rd of the frame. He is frowning and his lips are closed, but as scene progresses his lips move to a smile.

In this (YouTube) version the camera pans across to the women. Her head is turned to look at Lucy's father, but her eyes look to the camera. She gives a half smile and her left eyebrow moves to a 'raised' position. But these final seconds do not appear in the mainstream TV advert aired in Ireland.

Connotative readings: The music pauses for a moment and signifies 'dramatic effect'. It corresponds with Lucy's father's 'stare back' at Tom. This gaze changes from a serious, possibly disapproving expression, to a partial smile and then a crooked smile where one side of his mouth is smiling but the other side is not. This crooked smile functions to signify a sardonic expression, which is fleeting and incongruous. It is incongruous since we are now being asked as audiences to join 'the boy's club' in our attitude and standpoint with regard to the scene. A male gaze is positioning us in a heteronormative space. It is made further uncomfortable because we have been informed that this is Lucy's father and he seems to be colluding with Tom. The boy's club values supersede the parent-child relationship and the conventions that surround it.

The final shot which frames the mother does not appear in the Irish TV advert. However it is present in the online version of the text and that is the version being analysed so I am including it.

We are carried by binary codes that are acting as signifiers to identify the women with Lucy's dad as Lucy's mother. In a final incongruous moment she occupies the screen alone for the first time. She is framed off-centre, to the right. She looks to the camera, to the viewer, Tom, while holding her head to the side. She gives a hint of a smile, and raises her eyebrow in and expression that is so difficult to name that I asked a small sample of online readers to carry out a reading too. Below, see those readings:

> Admiration? a flirtatious look? Very odd. No anger or reprimanding going on. [It] could be 'that's my girl' [pride and approval]. (Female reader)
>
> [She may be thinking] You're a fine bit of stuff! But you're not pulling the wool over my eyes. (Female reader)
>
> It could be a 'and you are?' expression. (Female reader)
>
> [Her father] should have kicked him out! Or it could be a 'mmm Tom looks nice' [expression]. (Female reader)
>
> Aroused or proud. (Female reader)
>
> Impish/cheeky/little bit saucy? I think she's desiring him and approving of him as a partner. Not sure she's approving of her daughter, more her daughters choice in man. I also think it's a bit of a pleasant surprise, she wasn't expecting to be pleased. (Female reader)
>
> The expression could be 'world wise surmise', that is, been there, done that, got the T-shirt. You guys can't pull the wool over my eyes. As in 'the older, experienced woman', the knowing sideways glance. (Male reader)
>
> The expression is 'approving' but so is the father's. I imagine, though, that the expressions are directed at the boy, and they could also be interpreted as them thinking 'cool'. Which is how we're supposed to feel about the chewing gum, I guess. (Male reader)
>
> Hadn't seen the mother (grandmother?) reaction on TV – interesting to see if it was cut out or if I never noticed it. So chewing minty fresh Wrigley's will give us boys the confidence to face any situation and, who knows, older women will fancy you too? (Male reader)

And in a follow-up same respondent said:

> Just saw that odious Wrigley's ad on TV – no promiscuous mothers or raised eyebrows anywhere at the end, just the approving father.

Scene 11

Denotative reading: In the next shot we see a full screen of the product, with the words 'time to shine' in neon lights above the gum. The colour-scheme is blue to match the product's packaging.

Connotative readings: this is the only scene where the denotative and connotative readings may *coalesce. We are reminded of the product by name and by sight, and the product colours. The colour blue has western connotations of 'cool' and so the colour reinforces the message in the text. The gum = cool; and to chew it will be the embodiment of 'cool'. The final text message is 'Time to Shine' which is written in neon-tubing type and the words are illuminated to underline the 'shine' connotation.*

Other readings: 'Bring on the army of semioticians' (Williamson)

The small sample of readers gave their deconstructions of the advert in its entirety.

> That ad has ranked quite high on my 'most despicable ads' list for some time now. So that's how Wrigley's figure today's adolescent male brain operates. I might be offended if I was still one. (Male reader, March 2019)

> What strikes is the use of all shades of colour leading to the ultimate blue colour of the product: his boxers, jeans, her vest, the father's shirt, the mother's blue eyes there is also a balloon (?) in the background. All this is complemented and wrapped up in the complementary grey overall décor. Furthermore the combined colours of grey and blue are said to convey a sense of calmness which is ultimately illustrated in the bluish wrapping of the gum. Hence the message is that the gum is relaxing and calming as shown by the guy chewing it. (Male reader, March 2019)

> [There is a] sense of threat as the camera pans onto the door. The twist is when the guy asks for the jeans but not to put them on – for the gum. The gum is obviously the weapon here. The mum's appreciative look is easy to interpret – the dad's not as much. My reading of it is that that the dad is giving the guy the seal of approval because the guy is standing on his own two feet, is obviously quick thinking and has

> proven that he can 'protect' his daughter. It's almost as if the guy has opened the door with his gun drawn. (Female reader, March 2019)
>
> It seems like he is trying to impress the parents not her. (Female reader, March 2019)
>
> For me the gum box conveys the meaning of a box of condoms. Parents are impressed because the kids are responsible. (Female reader, March 2019)
>
> Never made sense to me but it's a bit racy for the audience that is aimed at, as in teens, preteens. (Female reader, March 2019)
>
> I think it's extremely sexist. There's obviously going to be a confrontation between him and the dad, so it conveys that if I eat this gum he'll think I'm cool and it works. The daughter and especially the mother are completely secondary. (Male reader, March 2019)
>
> This is all about male virility – even the mother raises her eyebrows in approval/attraction. Girl is secondary – oddly enough she has time to wear dungarees but he can only manage to open a gum. Her body is only seen by the boyfriend; he is free to stand around confident in his near nakedness. Father swayed by and approving of the kid's confidence, virility and suddenly no longer concerned for his daughter. All in all – charming [not!] (Female reader, March 2019)
>
> Places young man in power position and infers a silent code of masculinity and ownership of the young woman from father to new partner. Places young woman as passive player trying to please make role. Older woman further sidelined and marginalised as irrelevant to plot – just comedic scapegoat. (Female reader, March 2019)
>
> First impressions were there is some secret 'code' which made something deemed unacceptable, 'acceptable' and 'commendable' but since the woman, presumably the mother is also attracted to the gum user then it seemed more of a sexually powered phenomenon some sort of hyper-masculine sexual power. The strange ascetic father and older looking mother look repressed. I especially hated the artificial way the mother was aged: why would a woman who is no longer in her 20s or 30s be forcibly aged? Is it to remove her sexual attraction and make the reaction even more incredible – and funny? The way the incredulous daughter, fades into the background is also a further irritant. The women really get the short end of the stick here. (Female reader, March 2019)

The analyses from the 'army of semioticians' above, reinforces and add to the primary readings. They take critical standpoints, question the motives of the adverts producers, and recognize marketing strategies embedded in the texts.

Male-centred gazes

Most if not all of the gazes and looks in this advert are 'male-centred' gazes. They are either gazes carried out by men or they are gazes that position men as 'central'. They position the female in the story – Lucy – as a subject, and they draw a heteronormative gaze from the viewer.

Despite being identified at the beginning of the advert Lucy, the young female, remains in the background in both the advert and in the cultural recall. Interestingly Lucy never occupies the screen alone. Her boyfriend Tom is identified just before the end when he introduces himself. However in online searches and findings the advert is referred as 'Pants' and just as often as 'Tom' – not Lucy. This reinforces the 'male-centred' positioning of the audience through the framing of the characters and the connotative readings.

The gaze doesn't just function to positioning women as objects, there is a male to male gaze that also reduces woman to subject and then object. The Wrigley's/Orbit Ad does both. The conversation is 'about' the woman, but not as herself. It is about her as her role as object in a male-centred world. She is not presented with agency of any kind. Only the men in the advert have agency.

Traditional framings of the gaze, in advertising and everywhere else in the media, is around how 'she' looks, and subsequently how she is looked at. The rules of beauty, conformity and appearance apply and server to contain her body and her thinking about herself in relation to the world. This advert takes 'the gaze into another space. Lucy is the subject and the object of the gaze – the focus and the non-focus – she moves from being the spectacle to be looked at, to the object that is 'not looked at'.

The scripting of bodies ties in with the prevailing striptease culture and *Project Patriarchy and* about control through notions of perfection (Wolf 1990).

Women's everyday lived bodily experience are varied – the aim of this essay is to give words to meanings often unspoken, in ways that I hope evoke recognition and even a little bit of pleasure. In this essay I also engage in social criticism; and expose mundane ways that actions and opportunities for women are unfairly constrained by social norms regulating body comportment and by the needs of people for bodily care. This essay takes a feminist perspective, both as expressing sex- and gender-specific female subjectivity, and as claiming that women are not as free as we ought to be.

Scripting of selves: Dangerous discourses of freedom and pleasure

While women and girls and men and boys continue to take up their gendered scripts, they play the parts, follow the rules, and respond to the cues, entrances and exits without missing a beat. Ensuring that the status quo is not only adhered to and sustained, it remains unquestioned and unchallenged. The normalization of inequality persists, and the normalization of striptease cultures prevails. As readers/audiences/consumers we are continuously interpolated by mediatized portrayals in advertising (and beyond) of active boys and men: passive girls and women (Kilbourne), symbolic annihilation (Tuchman), silencing, invisibility and absences – alongside occupation stereotyping and boxing in, and out – reinforcing the 'you can do this, you can't do that; you can be this, you can't be that' social script.

When the social script *is* challenged, as the consciousness-raising writing within the second wave of feminism facilitated, and feminist media studies spotlighted the media sins around us, we are met with backlash. According to McRobbie (2011) a post-feminist backlash mitigated to undermine those feminist ideals, while at the same time selling ideas of empowerment, choice and individualism. In what she describes as a post-feminist context, it is possible for women to see themselves as empowered because they chose to buy painful expensive high-heel shoes, and spend money, time and effort transforming their appearance. Within with the current trend of Love Your Body marketing strategies, females are positioned to buy into the philosophy, and buy the products 'because they are worth it'. It is no longer successful for women to be 'body beautiful', they have to be beautiful *and* confident in mentality and attitude too. The traitorous and subversive discourses located in the Love Your Body campaigns is one where women must survey their own bodies and the self gaze needs to result in acceptance of self. A tricky tightrope for anyone to walk and yet when young women are asked why they wear 'the high heels, the uncomfortable clothes, the costly in time and money efforts of tanning and other body augmentations for perfection – the discursive practice has scripted a response of 'freedom of choice', of 'pleasure in the moment' and a love of self' and 'I'm worth it'.

Conclusions

Connell (1990: 523–7) talks about gender regimes where women and men occupy particular positions within the state, and work in ways structured by gender relations. This is the 'gender regime' defined as the historically produced state of play in gender relations within an institution, which can be analysed by taking a structural inventory. Three main structures can be identified – a gender division of labour; a structure of power, and the third component of a gender regime is the structure of cathexis, that is, the gender patterning of emotional attachments such as emotional labour. For Connell the way the state embodies gender gives it cause and capacity to 'do' gender.

The media functions within and is part of the ideological state apparatus and it plays its role to perfection. Gender regimes are reflected back to the actors and the scripts are regularly updated. The contemporary woman and girl is expected to perform what McRobbie (2009) refers to as a postfeminist masquerade where the well-educated working girl, the phallic girl and the global girl are roles and identities that are 'freely adopted' as statements of personal choice and empowerment. For her, the post-feminist masquerade functions in a sarcastic, quasi-feminist gesture, and by doing so wards off any potential threat to patriarchal authority. Hiding beneath this pretence of gender equality lies what McRobbie calls a 'provocation to feminism,' a 'triumphant gesture on the part of resurgent patriarchy' (2009: 85).

For Winch (2012) the hyper-visible landscape of popular culture enshrines a new feminine ideal, that is, the girl and the girled body. She is an asset, freed from the marriage market, and sold 'brand self'. Wince argues that the labour invested in the body is presented as 'me-time' and a normative body image is a signifier of success. Female friendships or 'girlfriendships' are exploited as women prove their worth through approval and praise of other women and are complicit in perpetuating discourses of misogyny. The reordering of body, with an updated set of ideals, valuation rules and demands for approval, re-places women and girls in a new but old role and performance. And while all this takes place, *Project Patriarchy* persists and prevails – but is now rendering itself invisible, as the liberation discourse is promoted and produced by the women and girls as they are subjected to new varieties of sexualization and objectification surface.

The mediatized aspects of *Project Patriarchy* harnesses the gaze. Whether it is an objectifying gaze by others or a self-surveillance, the self-policing that ensues is what Sandra Bartky famously coined 'a form of obedience to patriarchy' (Bartky, 1990, 80). In the opening quote I cite Young (2005: 3) who stated that 'the image of woman has not ceased being that of the Other: the surface that reflects fantasies and fears arising from our human being as vulnerable bodies'. The media from which the Wrigley's advert was created, is a reflection of this surface. The advert was produced by a creative team of men *and women* confirming what bell hooks articulated so beautifully 'patriarchy has no gender'. We are all part of *Project Patriarchy*; and just like any ideology, we have to step outside of it, to see, name it and resist it.

Bibliography

Advertising Standards (2018). *Case Report*. (Online), <https://adstandards.com.au/cases/2018/April?ref=0196/18>, accessed March 2019.

Althusser, L. (1971). 'Ideology and Ideological State Apparatuses'. In *Lenin and Philosophy, and Other Essays*. Trans. Ben Brewster. London: New Left Books. pp. 127–188.

Barthes, R. (1977). *Image, Music, Text.* New York: Hill and Wang.

Bartky, S. (1990). *Femininity and Domination: Studies in the Phenomenology of Oppression.* New York: Routledge.

Bordo, S. (1993). *Unbearable weight: Feminism, Western culture, and the body.* Berkeley: University of California Press.

Chandler, D. (2007). *Semiotics, The Basics.* London: Routledge.

—— (online) *Semiotics for Beginners.* <http://visual-memory.co.uk/daniel/Documents/S4B/sem06.html>, accessed March 2019.

Collins, R. L. (2011). 'Content Analysis of Gender Roles in Media: Where Are We Now and Where Should We Go?' *Sex Roles* (2011) 64: 290.

Connell, R. W. (1990). 'The State, Gender, and Sexual Politics: Theory and Appraisal'. *Theory and Society*, Vol. 19, No. 5 (October 1990), pp. 507–44.

—— (2005). *Masculinities.* Cambridge: Polity Press.

Fitzpatrick, M. J., and McPherson, B. J. (2010). 'Coloring Within the Lines: Gender Stereotypes in Contemporary Coloring Books', *Sex Roles* 62, 1–2; 127–37.

Foucault, M. (1963). *The birth of the clinic; an archaeology of medical perception.* New York: Pantheon Books, 1973. (Trans. A. M. Sheridan Smith. First published in French as *Naissance de la Clinique* (Paris: Presses Universitaires de France, 1963).)

—— (1975). *Discipline and punish: the birth of the prison.* New York: Pantheon Books.

Gauntlett, D. (2002). *Media, gender, and identity: an introduction.* London: Routledge.

Gerbner, G., and Gross, L. (1976). 'Living with Television: The Violence Profile', *Journal of Communication*, Volume 26, Issue 2, 1 June 1976.

Gill, R. (2007). *Gender and the Media.* Cambridge: Polity Press.

Grau, S. L., and Zotos, Y. C. (2016). 'Gender stereotypes in advertising: a review of current research', *International Journal of Advertising*, 35: 5, 761–70.

Hall, S. (1980). 'Encoding/Decoding'. In S. Hall, D. Hobson, A. Lowe, and P. Willis (eds), *Culture, Media, Language*, pp. 128–38. London: Hutchinson.

Hjarvard, S. (2013) *The Mediatization of Culture and Society*, London: Routledge.

hooks, b. (1992). *Black looks: Race and representation.* Boston, MA: South End Press.

—— (2010). *Teaching critical thinking: Practical wisdom.* New York: Routledge.

Horkheimer, M., and Adorno, T. W. (1972). *Dialectic of enlightenment.* New York: Herder and Herder.

Interview Magazine. 'Interview with Sia'. April 2015. <https://www.interviewmagazine.com/music/sia>, accessed February 2019.

Johnson, R. (1983). *What Is Cultural Studies Anyway?* Stencilled Occasional Paper, September 1983, General Series: SP No 74, Centre for Contemporary Cultural Studies: Birmingham.

Kaplan, E. A. (1996). *Looking for the Other: Feminism, Film, and the Imperial Gaze.* New York: Routledge.

Kilbourne, J. (1999). *Can't buy me love, How advertising changes the way we think and feel.* New York: Touchstone.

—— (2002). *Killing Us Softly 3, Advertising's Images of Women.* Northampton MA: Media Education Foundation.

Kimmel, M. S., Hearn, J., and Connell, R. W. (2005). *Handbook of studies on men & masculinities.* Thousand Oaks, CA: Sage.

Lutz, C. A., and Collins, J. L. (1991). 'The Photograph as an Intersection of Gazes: The Example of National Geographic'. In *Society for Visual Anthropology Newsletter.* March 1991.

—— (1994). 'The Photograph as an Intersection of Gazes: The Example of National Geographic'. In *Visualizing Theory.* Lucien Taylor, ed. pp. 311–39. New York: Routledge.

McNair, B. (2002). *Striptease Culture: Sex, Media and the Democratisation of Desire.* London: Routledge.

McRobbie, A. (2009). *The Aftermath of Feminism: Gender, Culture and Social Change.* London: Sage.

Murphy, B. (2015). *Brewing Identities: Globalisation, Guinness and the Production of Irishness.* New York: Peter Lang.

Portraying Politics: A toolkit on Gender and Television 2006 EU funded – <http://www.media-diversity.org/en/additional-files/documents/PP_EN.pdf>, accessed March 2019.

Pritchard, A., and Morgan, N. J. (2000). 'Privileging the male gaze: Gendered tourism landscapes'. *Annals of Tourism Research*, 27(4): 884–905.

Ross, K., Boyle, K., Carter, C., and Ging, D. (2016). 'Women, men and news: it's life, Jim, but not as we know it'. *Journalism Studies*, 19: 6, 824–45.

Said, E. (1991). *Orientalism.* London: Penguin.

Sturken, M., and Cartwright, L. (2009). *Practices of Looking: An Introduction to Visual Culture.* New York: Oxford University Press.

Thompson, N. (2016). *Anti-Discriminatory Practice: Equality, Diversity and Social Justice.* London: Palgrave.

Tuchman, G. (1978). 'The symbolic annihilation of women by the mass media'. In Tuchman G., Daniels, A. K., and Benet, J. (eds), *Hearth and home: Images of women in the mass media* (pp. 3–38). New York: Oxford University Press.

Turner, B. (1996). 'The Embodiment of Social Theory'. In *The Body and Society.* Sage: London.

Urry, J. (1992). 'The Tourist Gaze "Revisited"', *The American Behavioral Scientist*, 1 November 1992, 36, 2; ProQuest, p. 172.

—— (1992). 'The Tourist Gaze and the "Environment"'. *Theory, Culture & Society*, 9(3), pp. 1–26.

Williamson, J. (1988). *Decoding Advertising*. New York: Marion Boyars.

Winch, A. (2012). The girlfriend gaze. *Soundings*, Number 52, Winter 2012, pp. 21–32 (12).

Wolf, N. (1990). *The Beauty Myth: How Images of Beauty Are Used Against Women*. London: Chatto & Windus.

Young, I. M. (2005). *On Female Body Experience: 'Throwing Like a Girl' and Other Essays*. New York: Oxford University Press.

ISOBEL NÍ RIAIN

5 Nuala Ní Dhomhnaill's poetic women

In this chapter I will discuss Nuala Ní Dhomhnaill's poetic women. Ní Dhomhnaill questions the status quo. She sieves through folklore and Old Irish stories in her ongoing project to find the images, the language and the subversive potential that lend her poetry this power to demolish the taken for granted. By doing all of this she opens up a world of new possibilities. However, Ní Dhomhnaill is not always subversive. There are poems where she is quite content to accept the status quo, most notably, perhaps, in her work on the nurturing mother. This poet is a feminist but one who accepts the mother's role and relishes it. Seán Ó Tuama, in his seminal article on the *máthair ghrámhar* [the loving mother] and *máthair ghránna* [the bad mother] in Ní Dhomhnaill's poetry, sees the poet as expressing and transforming the woman inside herself. He seems to argue that Ní Dhomhnaill's poetry documents a very personal journey concerning her own life and voyage of self-discovery. I argue, in this chapter, that Ní Dhomhnaill is doing more than this; her poetic journey discloses a world which is inhabited by Irish women in general, and the work she does shines a light into the dark corners of Irish society.

I see Ní Dhomhnaill as working towards a Feminist Aesthetic. Sylvia Bovenschen maintained that in 1985 we had not arrived at a feminist aesthetic *per se*. We may not have arrived at such an aesthetic yet, but poets such as Nuala Ní Dhomhnaill are going in the right direction:

> I believe that feminine artistic production takes place by means of a complicated process involving conquering and reclaiming, appropriating and formulating, as well as forgetting and subverting ... Is there a feminine aesthetic? Certainly there is, if one is talking about aesthetic awareness and modes of sensory perception. Certainly not, if one is talking about an unusual variant of artistic production or about a painstakingly constructed theory of art. (Silvia Bovenschen 1985: 47–9)

We can find explanations of some of Ní Dhomhnaill's work in the psychological theories of Carl Gustav Jung. Jung writes about the fear the child experiences that he will be devoured by his mother. Bruno Bettelheim has written about the dread children experience that they will be devoured by the wicked witch, as seemed likely in 'Hänsel and Grettel', the wicked witch standing for the evil mother (Bettelheim 1981). It is noteworthy that while the poet Ní Dhomhnaill sees herself as the child at risk of being devoured by the evil mother – *an mháthair ghránna* – she sees herself as a loving mother.

Ní Dhomhnaill began writing poetry in her teens. Her early work is full of the fire and fury of the teenage girl. She takes personae from Irish mythology and radically alters the dynamics in the stories, pulling Medb, Mór Mumhan and the Mór-Ríon into the twentieth century. However, side by side with this tendency to subvert (Marcuse 1979: 6) the received wisdom of her time, is a tendency to go with the flow. I recently came across a reference in the book *The New Aestheticism*, where Joughin and Malpas state that modern art can be seen as 'suspended between subversion and complicity with the structures of domination' (Joughin and Malpas 2003: 53). Between 'subversion' and 'complicity' – perhaps every artist has to work out a compromise between these two forces. Nuala Ní Dhomhnaill is no exception.

In poems such as 'Fear' [Man], 'Gan do Chuid Éadaigh' [Without Your Clothes], 'Ag Cothú Linbh' [Feeding a Child], we see Nuala celebrating the status quo. She accepts the relationship between men and women, at a sexual level at any rate, and marvels at the baby in her arms in 'Ag Cothú Linbh'. The only 'subversion' we can see here is in 'Gan Do Chuid Éadaigh' when we find the poet objectifying the man and reducing him to an *oibiacht earótach* (Nic Dhiarmada 125) or erotic object. These men have no heads, no faces. They are sex-objects, sex-slaves. Maybe these poems are more subversive than at first appears.

The evil mother is jealous and spiteful in the poem 'Máthair' [Mother] from 'An Dealg Droighin'. The gifts that are given are taken back. Only one gift cannot be taken back, the life the mother has given the poet. The poet rebels surmising that she could tear the dress, drown the horse, destroy the harp and even take her own life. What would the mother say then? The poet thinks she would say the daughter was ungrateful (*míbhuíoch*), a schizophrenic. How different is this mother figure from the figure of the poet as mother portrayed in 'Ag Cothú Linbh' [Feeding a Child]. Here the mother figure breastfeeds her baby. She revels in the relationship between her baby and herself. Here is the loving mother par excellence, the *máthair ghrámhar* Seán Ó Tuama wrote about (Ó Tuama 1986). This mother-child relationship is seen as fundamental in the poem. It is the stuff that folktales are made of:

Is cé hiad pátrúin bhunaidh na laoch is na bhfathach munar thusa is mise? (*Rogha Dánta*,[1] 88)	And who are the original patterns of the heroes and giants if not you and I? (Trans. Michael Hartnett)

Writing poems about the mother, lashing out at what has long been an almost sacred figure in Irish society, this evil mother allows the young poet to give vent to her spleen. The poet sees herself as a loving mother, however, as seen in 'Ag Cothú Linbh' and 'Dán Do Mhelissa' [Poem for Melissa]. Occasionally, the poet identifies with the *máthair ghránna*. In the poem 'An Bhatráil' [The Battering] the poet seems to suggest that the main character in the poem is guilty of battering her children. Many topics addressed by Ní Dhomhnaill are taboo topics even now. In this poem, the poet portrays herself as a *máthair ghránna*. One wonders what is being disclosed here. Is the poet trying to see the point of view of mothers who abuse their children? The *lios* stands for a liminal space, a place between worlds, outside logic. It is the dream space of the unconscious. When the poet locates action in a *lios* setting, the reader cannot expect truth or rational arguments. The *lios* is the domain of imagination.

1 'RD' will stand for the work *Rogha Dánta* in this essay.

Thugas mo leanbhán liom aréir ón lios ar éigean.	I only just made it home last night with my child / from the fairy fort.
Bhí sé lán suas de mhíola is de chnathacha	He was crawling with lice and jiggers
(*The Astrakhan Cloak*,[2] 24–5)	(Trans. Paul Muldoon)

Is it any wonder that the *lios* is a place inhabited by women and dark forces in Ní Dhomhnaill's work. I imagine the *lios* to be a dark wet place, a womb like cavern. Angela Bourke discusses the importance of the *lios* and women's relation to it. The fairy folk, *slua sí*, have no women of their own according to the tradition (Bourke 1992: 81). They set about abducting women from the human domain at critical times in the women's lives. Those liminal times when the woman is newly married, or has just given birth or has miscarried are the times when the *slua sí* will strike. The woman will seem unlike herself for some reason, for reasons of post-natal depression, for example (82); her husband and his family will interpret this as the woman having been abducted and an *iarlais* or replacement being left in her place. Bourke gives the example where an ill woman was tortured to death on the fire by her in-laws in the mistaken belief that they would release the real woman from the *iarlais* (84).

To see Ní Dhomhnaill as only interested in exploring her own female essence ('*Tá Nuala ar thóir bhun-eisint na mná inti féin …*' Seán Ó Tuama (1986: 97)) is to neutralize the political and the radical potential inherent in her work. Celebrating female artists and poets as amazing individuals exploring their own womanhood independently of other women is to take the sting out of their art. Ní Dhomhnaill is not just talking about Nuala Ní Dhomhnaill. I would argue that she is every woman's poet. Ó Tuama seems to indicate this potential in Ní Dhomhnaill's work towards the end of his article when he speaks of mothers and children in general rather than the particular mother who is Nuala Ní Dhomhnaill (115). Bourke states boldly that Ní Dhomhnaill is making a stand for the women of Ireland

2 'AC' will stand for the work *The Astrakhan Cloak*.

in poems such as 'Fuadach' [Abduction] and 'Thar Mo Chionn' [On My Behalf] (Bourke 87).

According to Bourke the function of Art is to find a way to say the things that cannot be said or have never been said (89). It is indeed a form of disclosure which opens up new realms of meaning. Ní Dhomhnaill uses folklore and mythology to reclaim the past and in the process opens up the present. This opening up, this Universal World Disclosure, is part and parcel of the artist's task. Art is not a passive force in Herbert Marcuse's eyes. Art has the potential to bring about change not just at an Aesthetic level but at all levels of society:

> Art cannot change the world, but it can contribute to changing the consciousness and drives of the men and women who could change the world. (Marcuse 1979: 32)

Ní Dhomhnaill mixes the folkloric past with current news stories with references to the Second World War. Angela Bourke discusses the poem 'Thar Mo Chionn' [On My Behalf/Mea Culpa] (DF[3] 190–1) where the poet responds to the death of a young girl in a field who had just had a baby. It is an event I remember hearing about on the news when I was a school girl. In the poem 'An Traein Dubh' [The Black Train] (AC 28) Ní Dhomhnaill writes of the death camps of Nazi Germany. An atom bomb crops up in the poem 'An Ollmháthair Mhór' [Great Mother] (RD 58). Her ability to approach diverse topics and to open them up to poetic discourse within her own poetic world proves that Ní Dhomhnaill is not just a gifted individualist. Her range goes far beyond the personal. There is a political intent in her work that makes her internationally relevant.

I will now look at some of Ní Dhomhnaill's early work and its tendency to subvert. The Mór poems especially show the young Ní Dhomhnaill at her fieriest. Mór or Mór Mumhan is a figure from Irish mythology who is associated with kingship and going mad. Proinsias Mac Cana describes in detail Mór's history.[4] I see the poet talking to herself in the poem 'Mór

3 'DF' stands for the book *An Dealg sa bhFéar*.

4 Proinsias Mac Cana, 'Aspects of the Theme of King and Goddess in Irish Literature', *Études Celtiques* VII (1955), 78–80.

Goraí' [Mór Hatching]. She is creating for herself the persona of Mór. It is like a pep talk. Snap out of it, the poet is saying to herself.

'Mór Goraí'

Táimse á rá leat,
a Mhóir mhíchuibhseach,
go dtiocfaidh naithreacha uaithne
amach as do bholg
má fhanann tú ar gor
ar nimh na haithne
lá níos faide.

Cnuasaigh chugat isteach
Mar bheach
na huaireanta chloig a osclaíonn amach
fén ngréin rinn-ghathach;
aibíonn siad sa teas.
Bailigh iad
Is dein díobh
  laetha meala.
(RD 32–3)

'Mór Hatching'

I'm telling you,
unruly Mór,
that green snakes
will emanate from your womb
if you stay hatching
out this poisoned kernel
one day more.

Gather to your self,
like a bee,
the hours that are blossoming
in the sun's sharp sting:
they ripen in the heat.
Gather them –
From them create
  honeyed days.
(Trans. Michael Hartnett)

In the later poems, for example 'An Mhaighdean Mhara' [The Mermaid], the poet wrestles with the rise and fall of depressive illness. Perhaps as early as 'Mór Goraí' the 'nimh na haithne'/'poisoned kernel' can be seen as a trough of depression.

As a young poet, the Mór persona can be seen as functioning as a mask (Sewell 2002: 47), a way of saying what the poet wants to say but not being seen to be saying it. A young girl in the 1970s in Ireland talking about sexuality and sexual attraction may have found it necessary to hide behind a mythical figure such as Mór. In 'Dúil' [Desire] we have a very explicit description of sexual attraction but in the final line, there is a disownment of these feelings. It is Mór and not the poet who is feeling these sexual urges:

'Dúil'

An fear
lena mhealbhóg
ag cur ocrais orm;
na torthaí úra
fém' shúile
ag tarrac súlach
óm' cheathrúna
is an smuasach
        as croí mo chnámha;
        ag lagú
        mo ghlúine
        go titim.
        oop-la!
        barrathuisle,
        Mór ar lár.
(30–1)

'Dúil'

'This man
with his hamper
makes me hungry,
his fresh fruits
before my eyes
drawing juice
from my thighs
and marrow
        from my very joints
        weakening my knees
        to falling point.'

        Oop-la!
        She stumbles.
        Mór is down.
(Trans. Michael Hartnett)

The English translation makes use of quotation marks to clarify that this is not Nuala Ní Dhomhnaill's voice but rather Mór speaking. Máire Mhac an tSaoi describes this use of mythical figures as allowing Ní Dhomhnaill to explore her alter ego (Mhac an tSaoi 1988: 10–11). I don't see these personae as an 'alter' ego/egos so much as different aspects of the poetic voice. Perhaps we can say that Ní Dhomhnaill tries out possibly shocking subjects from within her mythological repertoire first and when she becomes courageous she can then speak boldly in the first person as she does in the poem 'Póg' [Kiss].

'Póg'

        Do phóg fear eile mé
i lár mo bheola,
do chuir sé a theanga

'Kiss'

        Straight on my mouth
another man's kiss.
He put his tongue

'Póg'

isteach i mo bhéal.
Níor bhraitheas faic.
Dúrt leis
'Téir abahile, a dheartháirín,

tán tú ólta
is tá do bhean thall sa doras
ag fanacht.'

Ach nuair a chuimním
ar do phógsa
critheann mo chromáin
is imíonn
a bhfuil eatarthu
ina lacht.

(38–9)

'Kiss'

Between my lips.
I was numb
and said to him
'Little man, go home

your wife waits at the door.'

But when I recall
your kiss
I shake, and all
that lies
between my hips
liquifies
to milk.
(Trans. Michael Hartnett)

In the poem 'Táimid Damanta A Dheirféaracha', Ní Dhomhnaill takes inspiration from the Russian poet Marina Tsvetayeva (Nic Dhiarmada 2005: 40). Ní Dhomhnaill's poem is very close to 'We Shall Not Escape Hell' by Tsvetayeva. Ní Dhomhnaill encourages women to go wild, to take to the sea in the nude, to risk censure from the clergy. Either way they are damned it would seem; damned to drudgery of keeping their husbands' house if they conform to social mores; damned by the Church and God himself, perhaps, if they follow their own desires and urges.

Táimid damanta, a dheirféaracha
sinne a chuaigh ag snámh
ar thránna istoíche is na réalta
ag gáirí in aonacht linn,
an mhéarnáil inár dtimpeall
is sinn ag scréachaíl le haoibhneas
is le fionnuaire na taoide,

We are damned, my sisters
we who swam at night
on beaches, with the stars
laughing with us
phosphorescence about us
we shrieking with delight
with the coldness of the tide

gan gúnaí orainn ná léinte	without shifts or dresses
ach sinn chomh naíonta le leanaí blianta,	as innocent as infants.
táimid damanta, a dheirféaracha.	We are damned, my sisters.
(14–15)	(Trans. Michael Hartnett)

Nic Dhiarmada quotes the translation of the Russian poem in full, I will give only the first verse:

> We shall not escape Hell, my passionate
> sisters, we shall drink black resins –
> we who sang our praises to the Lord
> with every one of our sinews, even the finest,
> (Trans. Elaine Feinstein; Nic Dhiarmada 2005: 40)

Ní Dhomhnaill exhorts Irish women to break free of their social, religious and domestic fetters and commune with nature as Tsvetayeva does also in her poem. Both poets warn women that the price of this freedom will be very high. In the poem 'Masculus Giganticus Hibernicus', Ní Dhomhnaill launches an attack on Irish men who sit in pubs plotting sexual intrigues:

Iarsma contúirteach ón Aois Iarainn,	Dangerous relic from the Iron Age
suíonn tú i bpubanna is beartaíonn	you sit in pubs and devise
plean gníomhaíochta an fhill	the treacherous plan
ná filleann,	that does not recoil on you –
ruathar díoltais ar an bhfearann	A vengeful incursion to female land.
baineann.	
(RD 78–9)	(Trans. Michael Hartnett)

Ní Dhomhnaill's early poems show clear signs of reclamation of the past and subversion of societal rules. I have focused only on early poems in this essay. As we can see, she is every woman's poet. She is particularly every Irish woman's poet. Her poetry is politically charged.

In the poem 'Teist Dhonncha Dí ar Mhór' (Donncha Di's Testimony), Ní Dhomhnaill puts herself in the shoes of Donncha Dí, one of Mór

Mumhan's consorts. It is perhaps a forerunner to the sentiments that play out in 'Leaba Shíoda' where the feminine body is extolled. Whilst 'Leaba Shíoda' is sometimes seen as a lesbian poem, 'Teist Dhonncha Dí ar Mhór' is supposedly spoken by Donncha Dí and, therefore, there appears to be no lesbian element here. Is this once again a camouflage giving the young poet licence to say whatever she wants by speaking through figures from the distant past?

'Teist Dhonncha Dí ar Mhór'

Do sheas sí lomnocht
Sa doircheacht.
a basa fuara – iasc gealúr –
ar mo ghuailne
a cromáin – tine ghealáin
faoi dhá ré a bruinne.

Thomas mo cheann
i bhfeamnach a gruaige;
bhí tonn ghoirt na sáile
am'bualadh, am'shuathadh;
ár gcapaill bhána ag donnú
ina bhfrancaigh mhóra.
gach aon ní ina chorcra.

Nuair a dhúisíos ar maidin bhí tinneas cinn orm.
Thugas fé ndeara
go raibh gainní an liathbhuí ag clúdach a colainne.
Bhí fiacla lofa an duibheagáin
ag drannadh orm.
Sea, thógas mo chip is mo mheanaithe
is theitheas liom.
(34)

'Donncha Di's Testimony'

She stood naked
in the dark,
her palms cold
like luminous fish

on my shoulders:
her hips
flashing fire
beneath the two moons
of her breasts.
 I sank my head
 in her sea-weed hair
 and bitter waves of sea
 bruised and battered me,
 our white-horse waves
 rusted to rats:
 all became empurpled.
In the morning waking
my head aching
I saw sallow scales encrusted her
and rotten teeth from the abyss
snarled at me and hissed.
I took my awl and last
and left the place fast!
(35 – trans. Michael Hartnett)

It seems that when Ní Dhomhnaill is at her most subversive she takes shelter in personae from mythology. The poetic use of characters from myth, transformed as they may be and speaking a modern message, give the poet licence to vent her spleen and yet not appear to be the speaker. In the poem 'Mór Cráite' [Mór Anguished], the poet makes mention of Mór's mental pain. Mór Mumhan lost her mind at one point in her traumatic history, but the poet generalizes the theme to include us all; we all being prisoners in our own private hells.

'Mór Cráite'

Tá Mór go dlúth fé ghlas
ina meabhairín bheag fhéin; 3"/4"/2"
ábhar liath is bán –

dearg (a bhíonn na créachta
a bháthann leath na gcuileanna
faid is a dheineann an leath eile a biaiste
ar fheoil na n-imeall)

'Éitíg', in ainm Dé,' ar sise leis na préacháin
is cabairí an Daingin a thagann san iarnóin
ag suathadh a mbolg.

'Tá na héinne dúnta isteach
ina ifreann féinín féin.'
Scaipeann na mion-éin
nuair a chuireann sí scrabhadh scraith
lastuas dóibh.
(36)

'Mór Anguished'

Mór, firmly under lock and key
in her own tiny mind
(2"x 4"x 3")
of grey, pinkish stuff
(here be the wounds
that drown the flies
while other flies survive
to make their maggots
on the carrion fringe).

'Listen, in God's name,' she begs
the magpies and the crows
that come at evening
to upset their guts,
'every one's enclosed
in their own tiny hells.'

The small birds
scatter and spread
when she flings up at them
a sod of earth.
(37 – Trans. Michael Hartnett)

The persona of Medb is invoked in later poems to castigate the men of Ireland. Easy sexual advances in pubs seem to be the main cause of the poet's ire in 'Labhrann Medb'. Ní Dhomhnaill has broached such subjects without the cover of mythological personae in 'Táimid Damanta a Dheirféaracha'. But that poem is heavily influenced by the Russian poet Marina Tsvetayeva's poem: 'We Shall Not Escape Hell.'[5] For now Ní Dhomhnaill is content to let Medb do the talking:

'Labhrann Medb'	'Medb Speaks'
Fógraím cogadh feasta	War I declare from now
ar fhearaibh uile Éireann,	on all the men of Ireland
ar na leaids ag na cúinní sráide	on all the corner-boys
is iad ina luí i lúib i gceas naíon,	lying curled in children's cradles
a bpilibíní gan liúdar	their willies worthless
is gan éileamh acu ar aon bhean	wanting no woman
ach le teann fearaíochta is laochais	all macho boasting
ag maíomh gur iníon rí Gréige	last night they bedded
a bhí mar chéile leapan aréir acu,	a Grecian princess –
is fógraím cogadh cruaidh feasta.	a terrible war I will declare.
(110–11)	(Trans. Michael Hartnett)

There is a nice reference to the love song 'Dónall Óg' in 'Labhrann Medhb'. '*Is iníon rí Gréige mar chéile leapa agat*' are the words from the original song.[6] It is not clear what exactly is meant by this reference to the Grecian king in the original love song. Perhaps it refers to the story 'Conall Gulban'.[7] In this story Conall marries the daughter of a Grecian king who was reputed to be the most beautiful woman in the world (226). Alternatively, it could simply be a reference to an exquisite lover. In the poem Labhrann Medb it is clearly their own masculine prowess that is meant by the men's supposed reference to the daughter of the Grecian king.

5 Bríona Nic Dhiarmada, *Téacs Baineann, Téacs Mná* (Dublin: An Clóchomhar Tta., 2005), 40.

6 Seán Ó Tuama, and Thomas Kinsella, eds, *An Duanaire 1600–1900: Poems of the Dispossessed* (Portlaoise: The Dolmen Press, 1985), 288, verse 1.

7 *Leabhar Sheáin Í Chonaill*, Ó Duilearga, ed., 1964: 222. I am indebted to Dr Seán Ó Duinnshléibhe for pointing me in the direaction of *Leabhar Sheáin Í Chonaill* for this interpretation of the reference to the daughter of a Grecian king.

It is the vulgar behaviour of the men of Ireland that disgusts Medb in the poem 'Labhrann Medb'.

Fógraím cath gan truamhéil	Merciless war I declare –
gan cur suas is gan téarmaí	endless, without quarter
ar laochra na bhfiche pint	on the twenty-pint heroes
a shuífeadh ar bhinse taobh liom,	who sit on seats beside me
a chuirfeadh deasláimh faoi mo sciortaí	who nicely up my skirts put hands
gan leathscéal ná gan chaoi acu	no apology or reason
ach iad ag lorg iarraim cúis	just looking for a chance
chun smacht a imirt ar mo ghéaga,	to dominate my limbs –
is fógraím cath gan truamhéil orthu.	a merciless war I will declare!
(110–11)	(Translated by Michael Hartnett)

Maryna Ramonets (2003) discusses Ní Dhomhnaill's treatment of Cú Chulainn and Medhb. Ramonets sees Ní Dhomhnaill's poetic Cú Chulainn as an attack on the version of manhood that the nationalists drew from in the lead up to and after 1916. The figure of the dying hero depicted in the sculpture of Cú Chulainn in the GPO in Dublin seems to imply that the uprising of 1916 was a very male affair and the subsequent role of women as home makers in the 1937 Constitution copper fastened the subordinate place of women in Irish society (Ramonets 2003: 58). Ramonets describes in detail Ní Dhomhnaill's Cú Chulainn who is depicted as a small, dark man who suffers from impotence (72). Ní Dhomhnaill turns the mythic Cú Chulainn on his head.

In the poem 'Cú Chulainn I', Ní Dhomhnaill seems to be rounding on Cú Chulainn as a representative of that mean bunch – the men of Ireland. It is a dissatisfactory poem in some ways. Why is Cú Chulainn a 'small rigid man' ('*A fhir bhig, dhoicht, dhorcha …*')? It is of course easier to dissect Cú Chulainn than to pick apart living men who may have angered the poet. Once again the poet is speaking from behind a persona from Irish myth. In the poem 'Cú Chulainn II', the child Cú Chulainn has permission to speak. He is sick of observing life being played out around him. He wants a part of the action. He asks his mother '*cé hé m'athair*?' – 'who is my father?' He doesn't get an answer. The old story is set in the present day. There is a cigarette in his mother's mouth. She is a single parent. It is a very common scenario in today's Ireland. The Cú Chulainn story gives the poet licence to speak on a subject that could be seen as controversial.

'Cú Chulainn II'

'A mháthair,' ol Cú Chulainn,
'raghad chun na macraidhe.
Inis dom cá bhfuilid
is conas raghad ann.
Táim bréan de bheith ag maireachtaint
ar immealbhoird bhur soalna,
caite i mo chnap ar leac thigh tábhairne
nuair a théann sibh ag ól pórtair,
ag crústadh cloch ar thraenacha
nó ag imirt póiríní le leanaí beaga,
ag féachaint ar na mairt á leagadh
nuair a bhíonn sibh ag búistéireacht
nó ar lasracha na dtinte cnámh
ag léimt sa tsráid go luath Oíche Shin Seáin.

Ach sara bhfágfad
cur uait do chniotáil
is bain an feaig as do bhéal neoimint,
abair liom aon ní amháin
is ná habair níos mó – a leithéid seo,
cé hé m'athair?'
D'fhéach Deichtine, a mháthair,
idir an dá shúil air.
D'oscail sí a béal chun rud a rá
ach dhún aríst é is ní dúirt sí faic.
Ní thugann mná tí stuama
freagra díreach ar cheist chomh dána léi.
Dá ndéanfadh seans go n-imeodh
an domhan mór uile ina raic.
(114)

'Cú Chulainn II'

'Mammy,' said Cú Chulainn,
'I will join the grown-ups.
Tell me where they are

and how I'll get to them.
I'm fed up living
on the edges of your lives
thrown in a heap on the pub doorstep
when you go drinking porter,
or tossing stones at passing trains
or marble-playing with kids
seeing the oxen falling
when you are butchering
or seeing the flames of bonfires
on St John's Eve.

But before I leave
put down your knitting
take the fag from your lip a minute
and tell me one thing –
who is my father?'

Deichtine his mother
stared at him
opened her mouth to speak,
closed it again, wordless.
No dedicated housewife would
answer such directness.
If word were said
the whole world would be
in chassis.
(Translated by Michael Hartnett)

Ní Dhomhnaill often uses personae from myth and folklore to speak for her. Others have seen both myth and folklore as endowing the poet with 'material, methods, and means of subtly and suggestively expressing or dramatizing a range of contemporary personal and universal conflicts' (Sewell 2002: 42). The two interpretations are not mutually exclusive. I merely see the poet as allowing the personae from myth and folklore to speak for the poet and thus give her licence to say things that she may not feel comfortable saying in her own poetic voice. The role of transformation in Ní Dhomhnaill's use of the past in her poetry recurs repeatedly in discussions of her work. This element was commented on some years ago by Seán Ó Tuama. He called it a '*claochló*' which is the Irish word for transformation (Ó Tuama 1986: 95). Ó Tuama maintained that a poet needs to carry out a personal transformation of the material s/he is working with. We can say that all poets need to perform a poetic transformation of both everyday material and of the mythic material that some select to use in their work. It is only by transforming that one creates poetry from the mundane. The mythic will have no relevance to modern-day life unless it is transformed.

In the poem 'Agallamh na Mór-Ríona le Cú Chulainn' (The Great Queen speaks. Cú Chulainn Listens.), one could infer that the poet is subverting the taken-for-granted relationship between the hero and the heroine of ancient myth. To an extent she is. However, I cannot help getting the impression that the Mór-Ríon is simply a woman scorned venting her spleen. And one wonders what is subversive about this. However, the woman here has power. She has the power to bestow kingship as did the other goddesses associated with sovereignty in Old Irish mythology:

'Agallamh na Mór-Ríona le Cú Chulainn'	'The Great Queen Speaks. Cú Chulainn listens'
Do thángas-sa chughat i bhfoirm ríona, éadaí ildaite orm agus cuma sciamhach, le go mbronnfainn ort cumhacht agus flaitheas tíre, an dúiche inmheánach ina hiomláine, críocha uile an anama i nóiméad aimsire, a bhforlámhas uile is a nglóir siúd mar is ar mo láimh a tugadh é chun é a bhronnadh ar cibé is áil liom. Thugas chughat mo sheoda is mo chuid eallaigh. (116)	I came to you as a queen colourfully clothed beautifully formed to grant you power and kingdoms all the internal country all the territory of the soul in one second power over all this and much glory for it was given to me to bestow on whom I wish I brought you jewellery And chattels. (117 – trans. Michael Hartnett)

Irish men are an easy target for an Irish female poet. Ní Dhomhnaill strikes out at them directly in 'Masculus Giganticus Hibernicus':

> Iarsma contúirteach ón Aois Iarainn,
> suíonn tú i bpubanna is beartaíonn
> plean gníomhaíochta an fhill
> ná filleann,
> ruathar díoltais ar an bhfearann baineann.
> (78)
>
> Dangerous relic from the Iron Age
> you sit in pubs and devise
> the treacherous plan
> that does not recoil on you –
> a vengeful incursion to female land.
> (79 – trans. Michael Hartnett)

Ní Dhomhnaill attacks Cú Chulainn's inability or unwillingness to satisfy the sexual urges of the Mór-Ríon in the poem discussed above, 'Agallamh na Mór-Ríona le Cú Chulainn':

Ach nuair a shleamhnaíos
'on leabaidh chughat
dúraís, 'Cuir uait!
Ní tráth imeartha í seo.
Ní ar son tóin mná
a tugadh ar talamh mé!
Bhí an domhan mór uile
le bodhradh fós
le do ghníomhartha gaile,
bhí barr maise
le cur ar do ghaisce,
is do thugais droim láimhe orm
murar thugais dorn iata.
All right, mar sin,
bíodh ina mhargadh,
beatha dhuine a thoil.
(116)

But when I slipped
into bed with you
you said 'Get off!'
This is no time for fun
I'm not here on behalf
of a woman's bum!
The wide world was yet
to be deafened
by your great deeds
your skills had yet
to be improved
and you gave me the back of your hand
If you didn't a closed fist.
All right, so –
it's a bargain –
please yourself.
(117 – Michael Hartnett)

Is Cú Chulainn above just another Irish male? Or does he represent all of Irish manhood? Cú Chulainn, known for his prowess and irresistible attraction to women, comes in for a mocking and a berating from Ní Dhomhnaill. It is odd that Ní Dhomhnaill doesn't take a look at Irish women and see if they are not material for a similar type of poetic treatment. The right to say no to sexual advances seems to be a right men do not share with women in this poetry.

Sexual mores and sexual desires are not easy subjects to write about even in today's Ireland. Ní Dhomhnaill takes the bull by the horns. However, she speaks through her mythological personae in many poems. It is undeniably more comfortable to do so than to speak from the first person singular position. She rebukes her male characters. She objectifies her male lovers. One wonders how women would fair if she gave them the same treatment poetically. Is Ní Dhomhnaill's method a good way to redress the historical imbalance that has treated women as the subject matter if not the subjects of poetry?

Art 'transcends' everyday life. Art can thereby 'subvert' our daily experience (Marcuse 1979: 6). One of the ways that poets can subvert that everyday experience is not just in their choice of subjects but importantly in their use of language. By using words from different dialects and words that are not in Ó Dónaill's dictionary, bible of Modern Irish, Ní Dhomhnaill leaves us to wonder. We have to accept some words from their context and just go with the flow. Other Irish poets, such as Biddy Jenkinson, use obscure Irish words that make us scratch our heads. Poets use language in strange ways. This strangeness can be seen as causing 'estrangement' (Marcuse 9–10). Art is not a passive force in Marcuse's eyes. Art has the potential to bring about change not just at an aesthetic level but at all levels of society (32).

The importance of language and the transformative potential of poetic discourse cannot be underestimated. According to Marcuse there is a need for everyday life to undergo aesthetic 'formation', a type of 'stylization' that raises everyday reality to the level of aesthetic reality (44). What Ní Dhomhnaill and Jenkinson do with the Irish language, by twisting and turning old and new phrases and drawing from the English language and the classical past of the Irish language, they transform the everyday. This 'formation' allows them to analyse, critique and subvert everyday Irish society.

Portraying women in new ways, using Irish myth in ways that question and even attack the received norms involved in social relationships, particularly between men and women, opens up a vision of an alternative reality. The Aesthetic Domain is deeply involved in what critical theorists term Universal World Disclosure. Ní Dhomhnaill's poetry sometimes takes part in this type of disclosure. She has certainly opened up a space within the Irish language where new discussions can take place. She has extended the field of reference of Irish-language poetry.

Art 'creates the realm in which the subversion of experience proper to art becomes possible' (Marcuse 1979: 6). Women's experience of the everyday is surely experience proper to art. As we have seen, Ní Dhomhnaill subverts the status quo and complies with it. One of my students commented that it was impossible to get a general feeling for Ní Dhomhnaill's work, a general theory that would cover it. I agree, the more one reads of Ní Dhomhnaill, the more different ideas come to mind. Ní Dhomhnaill is doing different things in different poems. Her point of view is constantly shifting. She sees problems in modern Irish society through the prism of Irish mythology which she reworks to fit her poetic project. She estranges characters from mythology, bringing them into the contemporary era, and she estranges contemporary reality by bringing elements of the tradition to bear. She brings about a transformation – a '*claochló*' in Seán Ó Tuama's words. She creates in the process an authentic poetic voice and she provides views of Irish society that startle, amuse and make us at times question the status quo and all of this through the medium of the Irish language.

Bibliography

Bettelheim, Bruno (1981). 'Fairy Tales as Ways of Knowing', in Michael M. Metzger and Katharina Mommsen, eds, *Essays on Märchen in Psychology, Society and Literature* (*Germanic Studies in America*, No. 41) (Bern: Peter Lang), 11–20.

Bourke, Angela (1992). 'Bean an Leasa: Ón bPiseogaíocht go dtí Filíocht Nuala Ní Dhomhnaill', in Eoghan Ó hAnluain, ed., *Leath na Spéire* (Dublin: An Clóchomhar Tta.), 74–90.

de Paor, Pádraig (1997). *Tionscnamh Filíochta Nuala Ní Dhomhnaill* (Dublin: An Clóchomhar).

Bovenschen, Sylvia (1985). 'Is there a Feminine Aesthetic?' in Gisela Ecker, ed., *Feminist Aesthetics* (London: The Women's Press), 23–50.

Joughin, John J., and Malpas, Simon (2003). *The New Aestheticism* (Manchester: Manchester University Press).

Mac Cana, Proinsias (1955). 'Aspects of the Theme of King and Goddess in Irish Literature', *Études Celtiques* VII, 76–114.

Marcuse, Herbert (1979). *The Aesthetic Dimension* (London: The MacMillan Press Ltd).

Ní Dhomhnaill, Nuala (1988). *Rogha Dánta*, trans. Michael Hartnett (Finglas: The Raven Arts Press).

—— (1991). *Feis* (Maynooth: An Sagart).

—— (1992). *The Astrakhan Cloak*, trans. Paul Muldoon (Co. Meath: The Gallery Press).

—— (2011). *An Dealg sa bhFéar* (Co. Galway: Cló Iar-Chonnacht).

Nic Dhiarmada, Bríona (2005). *Téacs Baineann Téacs Mná* (Dublin: An Clóchomhar Tta.).

Ó Duilearga, Séamus, collector and ed. (1964). *Leabhar Sheáin Í Chonaill – Scéalta agus Seanchas Ó Íbh Ráthach* (Dublin: Brún agus Ó Nualláin Teoranta).

Ó Tuama, Seán (1986). 'Filíocht Nuala Ní Dhomhnaill "An Mháthair Ghrámhar is an Mháthair Ghránna" ina cuid filíochta' in Pádraig Ó Fiannachta, ed., *Léachtaí Cholm Cille XVII* (Maynooth: An Sagart), 95–116.

Ó Tuama, Seán, and Kinsella, Thomas, eds (1985). *An Duanaire 1600–1900: Poems of the Dispossessed* (Portlaoise: Dolmen Press).

Romanets, Maryna (2003). 'Degenerating the Myth of Transhistorical Masculinity: Nuala Ní Dhomhnaill's Cú Chulainn Cycle.' *Nordic Irish Studies* 2 =, 57–74. <https://www-jstor-org.ucc.idm.oclc.org/stable/pdf/30001487.pdf?refreqid=excelsior%3Aacc65347d18ea8529a7ddd91e8d00800>, accessed 19 September 2017.

Sewell, Frank (2002). 'Irish Mythology in the Early Poetry of Nuala Ní Dhomhnaill.' *Hungarian Journal of English and American Studies* (HJEAS), 8/1, 39–56.

Permissions

Extracts from The Astrakhan Cloak by Nuala Ní Dhomhnaill translated by Michael Hartnett are reproduced by kind permission of the author, the Estate of Michael Hartnett and The Gallery Press. <http://www.gallerypress.com>.

Index

PETER LANG
PROMPT

Peter Lang Prompts offer our authors the opportunity to publish original research in small volumes that are shorter and more affordable than traditional academic monographs. With a faster production time, this concise model gives scholars the chance to publish time-sensitive research, open a forum for debate, and make an impact more quickly. Like all Peter Lang publications, Prompts are thoroughly peer reviewed and can even be included in series.

For further information, please contact:

Published by Peter Lang Ltd,
International Academic Publishers,
52 St Giles, Oxford,
OX1 3LU, United Kingdom

To order, please contact our Customer Service Department:

oxford@peterlang.com

Visit our website: www.peterlang.com

Prompts include:

Claudia Aburto Guzmán, *Poesía reciente de voces en diálogo con la ascendencia hispano-hablante en los Estados Unidos: Antología breve*. ISBN 978-1-4331-5207-8. 2020

Tywan Ajani, *Barriers to Rebuilding the African American Community: Understanding the Issues Facing Today's African Americans from a Social Work Perspective*. ISBN 978-1-4331-7681-4. 2020

Marcilio de Freitas and Marilene Corrêa da Silva Freitas, *The Future of Amazonia in Brazil: A Worldwide Tragedy*. ISBN 978-1-4331-7793-4. 2020

Janet Farrell Leontiou, *The Doctor Still Knows Best: How Medical Culture Is Still Marked by Paternalism*. Health Communication, vol. 15. ISBN 978-1-4331-7322-6. 2020

Clare Gorman (ed.), *Miss-representation: Women, Literature, Sex and Culture*. ISBN 978-1-78874-586-4. 2020

Eva Marín Hlynsdóttir. *Gender in Organizations: The Icelandic Female Council Manager*. ISBN 978-1-4331-7729-3. 2020

Micol Kates, *Towards a Vegan-Based Ethic: Dismantling Neo-Colonial Hierarchy Through an Ethic of Lovingkindness*. ISBN 978-1-4331-7797-2. 2020

Josiane Ranguin, *Mediating the Windrush Children: Caryl Phillips and Horace Ové*. ISBN 978-1-4331-7424-7. 2020

Dylan Scudder, *Coffee and Conflict in Colombia: Part of the Pentalemma Series on Managing Global Dilemmas*. ISBN 978-1-4331-7568-8. 2020

Dylan Scudder, *Conflict Minerals in the Democratic Republic of Congo: Part of the Pentalemma Series on Managing Global Dilemmas.* ISBN 978-1-4331-7561-9. 2020

Dylan Scudder, *Mining Conflict in the Philippines: Part of the Pentalemma Series on Managing Global Dilemmas.* ISBN 978-1-4331-7632-6. 2020

Dylan Scudder, *Multi-Hazard Disaster in Japan: Part of the Pentalemma Series on Managing Global Dilemmas.* ISBN 978-1-4331-7530-5. 2020

Shai Tubali, *Cosmos and Camus: Science Fiction Film and the Absurd.* ISBN 978-1-78997-664-9. 2020

Angela Williams, *Hip Hop Harem: Women, Rap and Representation in the Middle East.* ISBN 978-1-4331-7295-3. 2020

Ivan Zhavoronkov (trans.), *The Socio-Cultural and Philosophical Origins of Science* by Anatoly Nazirov. ISBN 978-1-4331-7228-1. 2020

www.ingramcontent.com/pod-product-compliance
Lightning Source LLC
Chambersburg PA
CBHW070627310726
48982CB00001B/188
* 9 7 8 1 7 8 8 7 4 5 8 6 4 *